S0-AFN-041

7104

kaiserschlacht 1918

the final german offensive of world war one

RANDAL GRAY

kaiserschlacht 1918

the final german offensive of world war one

Praeger Illustrated Military History Series

PRAEGER

Westport, Connecticut
London

Library of Congress Cataloging-in-Publication Data

Gray, Randal.
    Kaiserschlacht 1918: the final German offensive of World War One / Randal Gray.
       p. cm – (Praeger illustrated military history, ISSN 1547-206X)
    Originally published: Oxford: Osprey, 1991.
    Includes bibliographical references and index.
    ISBN 0-275-98289-0 (alk. paper)
    1. Somme, 2nd Battle of the, France, 1918. I. Title. II. Series.
    D545.S75G73   2004
    940.4'34–dc22   2003063219

British Library Cataloguing in Publication Data is available.

First published in paperback in 1991 by Osprey Publishing Limited, Elms Court,
Chapel Way, Botley, Oxford OX2 9LP. All rights reserved.

Copyright © 2004 by Osprey Publishing Limited

Library of Congress Catalog Card Number: 2003063219
ISBN: 0-275-98289-0
ISSN: 1547-206X

Praeger Publishers, 88 Post Road West, Westport, CT 06881
An imprint of Greenwood Publishing Group, Inc.
www.praeger.com

Printed in China through World Print Ltd.

The paper used in this book complies with the Permanent Paper Standard issued
by the National Information Standards Organization (Z39.48-1984).

10 9 8 7 6 5 4 3 2 1

FRONT COVER: courtesy of the Imperial War Museum, London

CONTENTS

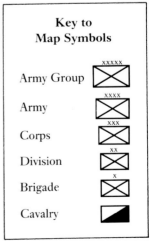

Key to Map Symbols

Army Group	xxxxx
Army	xxxx
Corps	xxx
Division	xx
Brigade	x
Cavalry	

THE ORIGINS OF THE BATTLE

The German spring offensive of 1918, above all Ludendorff's offensive, wears many names, but none more appropriate than Kaiserschlacht ('Emperor's battle'), the name bestowed on it by General der Infanterie Erich Ludendorff in honour of his sovereign and supreme warlord Kaiser Wilhelm II. It conveys the grim, titanic grandeur of the event, nothing less than the First World War's greatest single attack (unless one regards the German August 1914 march west as a single battle). Like that original Schlieffen Plan, Kaiserschlacht was a gamble for quick victory before superior Allied resources could be brought into play.

Some sources also call it the *Friedensturm* ('Peace Offensive') as a cynical attempt by Ludendorff to motivate his soldiers' efforts. This term only properly applies as the codename of Ludendorff's fifth and final 1918 blow, his Marne–Reims offensive of July (Second Battle of the Marne) when the German Army's final, flagging effort needed every possible inspiration.

For the British the battle has never really had a satisfactory name. In the official nomenclatures, 'First Battles of the Somme 1918' invites confusion with the 1916 battles forever seared into the national consciousness. The battle nomenclature committee's sequence then continues: Battle of St. Quentin; First Battle of Bapaume; Actions at Somme Crossing; Battle of Rosières; First Battle of Arras 1918; British Battle of the Avre; and Battle of the Ancre 1918. These are perfectly sensible subdivisions, although Amiens is ignored, but scarcely do justice to what was the greatest and most intense battle ever fought by the British Army. Second Battle(s) of the Somme is a much clearer and more memorable description, although geographically the fighting extended north of Arras (Artois). Instead these events are perhaps best called to mind, with that typically perverse

British love of defeats, as the 'Great March Retreat'.

For the French the fighting raged as the 'Second Battle of Picardy' with the successive battles of 'Noyon' and 'the Avre' (differently dated from the British one). For the Germans it was simply the 'Grosse Schlacht in Frankreich', the Great Battle in France.

Whatever we otherwise call Kaiserschlacht, it certainly represented the most awful non-nuclear (but chemical) fighting ordeal undergone by twentieth century soldiers, with the possible exception of some 1941-5 Eastern Front battles and the Iran-Iraq War.

Germany had escaped the two-front nightmare of Graf von Schlieffen courtesy of the two 1917 Russian revolutions. In 1915 she had eliminated Serbia from the Allied line-up; in 1916 Roumania; and by September 1917 Russia was militarily impotent with the fall of Riga and under a Bolshevik-menaced provisional government. In October seven crack German divisions formed into General der Infanterie Otto von Below's Austro-German Fourteenth Army had broken the long Italian Front stalemate by mountain infiltration tactics and had flung the Italian Army 70 miles back to the Piave with the loss of 325,000 prisoners in the rout known as Caporetto (from the point at which Below broke through).

In the winter of 1917/18 the Western Front remained 468 miles of entrenched deadlock between four major armies, now becoming five. In the far north the Belgians still clung to the 23-mile remnant of their homeland by the Channel coast. The British Expeditionary Force (BEF) held the central 116 miles of the front in Flanders and Picardy. The French Army, recovering from the mutinies of early 1917, under Général de Division Henri Pétain's judicious leadership, held a line twice that length but not to the same density. And, by the end of 1917, the much heralded US Army had almost 184,000 personnel in France, but as of 31 January 1918 held precisely six miles of the front with one formed combat division. Dependent on British shipping and French-manufactured heavy equipment, the US commander, General John J. Pershing, had orders to fight as an independent army exactly as the original BEF had in 1914; his remaining troops were training. In the wake of Russia's revolution, both the Allies and the Central Powers saw the Americans as a fresh addition to the European deadlock. At least half a million more men were expected in the coming year.

It was at this juncture that General der Infanterie Erich Ludendorff's mind turned to an offensive in the West. He knew that neither the German Army, impressive though its defensive successes had been, nor the Central Powers' allies could stand another grim year on the defensive like 1917. Politically, France was recovering vigour under her new 76-year-old prime minister, the remarkable Georges Clemenceau, whose rhetoric and recall to office seemed vividly to anticipate Churchill's in 1940. To Ludendorff it was unthinkable that Germany, having defeated all the eastern and southern Entente powers, should treat with the Western allies at the very time the Brest Litovsk peace talks were ending any threat from Russia. Besides, after 3½ years of sacrifices, the Allies were not offering terms acceptable to Germany.

▼ *German infantry columns marching towards the front in Picardy. Horse-drawn transport is visible between the first company and the second. In less than four months (from 30 November 1917) 42 divisions (34 from the Eastern Front and Roumania), more than 500,000 troops, reinforced the Western Front.*

THE OPPOSING COMMANDERS

The German Commanders

By the time Ludendorff unleashed Kaiserschlacht on the BEF, his famous command partnership with Feldmarschall Paul von Hindenburg had lasted three and a half years. The relationship was so close that the Kaiser himself referred to the 'Siamese Twins' when the combination finally split in defeat the following autumn. This pairing was much more than the military one originally established at Tannenberg. Since July 1917 Hindenburg and Ludendorff's 'silent dictatorship' now ran not only Imperial Germany but also effectively the Central Powers as a whole. It is too easy to see Ludendorff as the directing brain for decisions and operations in the name of a 70-year-old field marshal who was little more than a figurehead – Hindenburg gave Kaiserschlacht's purpose and preparation his immense moral authority both at home and at the front. It was for him, rather than for Ludendorff or the Kaiser, that the German Army and people would make a final bid for victory in the West.

Two of the army commanders chosen by Ludendorff to be his executants were probably the best available to Imperial Germany. Significantly, all three had served on the Eastern Front in successful large-scale offensive operations directed by Hindenburg and himself. Furthermore, all had Western Front experience: General

▶Erich Ludendorff (1865-1937), who never received the ennobling Von, was convinced that only his Kaiserschlacht plan offered Germany victory; the alternative, as he told Prince Max of Baden in February 1918, was annihilation. He believed that the Army was 'pining for the attack' and that a succession of attacks would unlock the Western Front. ▶Below: Paul von Hindenburg (1849-1934) as Chief of Staff was practically a grandfather figure to the nation and no less convinced that a spring offensive was the only option.

▶ *The Commander and staff of the German Eighteenth Army in jaunty mood at their HQ in April 1918. General der Infanterie Oskar von Hutier (1857-1933) is second from the left next to his chief of staff, Generalmajor von Sauberzweig. Both generals wear the* Pour le Mérite *and Iron Cross. Sauberzweig had shrewdly predicted in an appreciation of 16 January that the French would not rush to help the BEF. After Kaiserschlacht, the French misleadingly complimented Hutier by calling the new German offensive methods 'Hutier tactics'. These were actually the work of many German officers from.*

der Kavallerie Georg von der Marwitz and General der Infanterie Oskar von Hutier as formation leaders in 1914's early rapid advances; Below as Sixth Army commander during the 1917 defensive Battle of Arras (in the same sector in which he was now about to attack). Marwitz had defended his Cambrai sector since December 1916 and directed the successful counterblow to the surprise British tank assault of November 1917.

No less important in the German system of command were the chiefs of staff. They handled administrative and tactical details but also took command decisions in their chiefs' absence. Hutier's reputation as victor of Riga owed much to his chief of staff, Generalmajor von Sauberzweig, as did Below of Italy to the able Bavarian Krafft von Dellmensingen. Marwitz, on the other hand, had a new chief of staff only a month before the offensive was to be launched. At army group level, Generalleutnant Hermann von Kühl and Oberst Graf Friedrich von der Schulenberg were the real intermediaries between the armies and Ludendorff, rather than their exalted crown prince superiors.

The fourteen corps commanders stand out from the usual obscurity of that level in the German Army. Three at least had commanded

▲ *General der Kavallerie Georg von der Marwitz (1856-1929), Commander of the German Second Army, seated with his chief of staff standing. The* latter is probably Oberstleutnant Stapff, who was replaced less than a month before Kaiserschlacht.

▲*General der Infanterie Otto von Below (1857-1944) commanded the Seventeenth Army from 1 February 1918 after the most varied and successful service of any German army commander, beginning with command of I Reserve Corps at Gumbinnen and*

Tannenberg during August 1914. His elder brother, Fritz, was also a Western Front army commander (since April 1915); another, Eduard, commanded VIII Corps in Alsace, while a younger one, Hans, commanded 238th Division, which made the record advance on 21 March.

▲*Field Marshal Sir Douglas Haig (1861-1928) took 48 hours to appreciate the scale and success of Kaiserschlacht, but his advocacy of Foch as Generalissimo was a turning-point for the Allied cause. He offered his resignation on 6 April 1918, but Secretary of State for War Lord Derby*

declined to accept it. There was no obvious alternative candidate.

large independent attacking groups in the 1916 Carpathian mountain campaigns against Russia and Roumania. Another, General der Infanterie H. von Kathen, had actually directed the October 1917 Baltic amphibious seizure of the islands across the Gulf of Riga, piquantly code-named 'Albion'. For Kaiserschlacht, as at Cambrai, each corps commander had between three and seven divisions to control instead of the usual two or three.

The Allied Commanders: BEF

At the beginning of 1918, Field Marshal Sir Douglas Haig's reputation stood at its lowest ebb. The protracted butchery of the Third Battle of Ypres was having its impact at home, to the extent

that his army, with five good divisions diverted to prop up Italy, was being denied adequate replacements by Lloyd George. The bright promise of the tank blow at Cambrai had dissolved into recriminations over a half-defeat and an ugly court of inquiry that blamed the troops. In January, Lloyd George's emissaries crossed the Channel to canvass vainly for Haig's successor. The Chief of the Imperial General Staff, General Sir William Robertson, Haig's bulwark at home, had been removed (in February) after opposing a complex intrigue over control of Allied reserves, to be replaced by the arch-political intriguer and Francophile, General Sir Henry Wilson.

Pressure within the Army hierarchy forced Haig to change his long-serving Chief and Deputy Chiefs of Staff, over-optimistic Intelligence head, and over-age Quarter-Master General either side of the New Year. In the long run, these changes would be beneficial, but in the weeks for preparing defences to meet Kaiserschlacht such upheavals at General Headquarters hardly strengthened its already tarnished authority.

Yet appearances can be deceptive. Haig's much derided lack of imagination may even have helped at this period. His personal morale was unaffected – indeed positively strengthened. On 2 January, a year after promotion, he received his field marshal's baton from the King at Buckingham Palace. On 15 March, six days before Ludendorff struck, Lady Haig gave birth to their first child, a son (the present Earl Haig). This apparently private matter takes on added significance when it is realized that his adversary was to lose a second stepson to British action in the first days of his offensive and to visit the grave.

Haig's confidence was best expressed to his wife on 28 February: 'in the words of 2nd Chronicles XX chap, that it is "God's battle" and I am not dismayed by the numbers of the enemy'. Three days later his only fear was that the BEF's defences would make Ludendorff hesitate.

The Army commanders tasked with repelling it lacked this lofty certainty. General Sir Julian Byng of Third Army had planned the Cambrai tank thrust only to be caught out by the German riposte. Now he stubbornly refused to shorten his front by giving up the 'Byng boys' remaining gain, the awkward Flesquières salient. General Sir Hubert Gough, of all the 'barons', as the BEF's Army commanders were known, had the most thankless task on the longest and newest front, with a Fifth Army only recently brought together again. Furthermore, at Haig's insistence, his personal friend and long-standing but much criticized Chief of Staff, Major-General Neil Malcolm, was switched to the command of 66th

▲General Sir Julian Byng (1862-1935), commander of Third Army since June 1917, did not shine against Kaiserschlacht, but he did accurately report the two sides' mutual exhaustion on the morning of 26 March. Thereafter Anzac and other reserves stiffened his line.

▲General Sir Hubert Gough (1870-1963) of Fifth Army, the youngest (since May 1916) and unluckiest army commander on either side. Lloyd George was determined to recall him, and a proposed inquiry into his army's fate was never held. Gough published his own account The Fifth Army in 1931.

Division, the last to arrive in France. Gough's choice for replacement was refused, and his deputy QMG was changed in like fashion. These appointments reflected Gough's own tenuous status via unfavourable perceptions of his 1917 performance at Ypres. By early March, the War Minister was writing to Haig that the Government and indeed Fifth Army lacked confidence in Gough and his staff. He stayed, however, his terrier-like fighting qualities known to Haig and to many of the soldiers he commanded.

Eight corps commanders would fight the defensive battle ahead in a crucial tactical sense. Were they qualified? No fewer than six of them had commanded brigades or larger formations in the original BEF during the desperate defensive fighting of 1914. Five had commanded divisions or

corps in the 1916 Somme battles. Only two could be said to lack corps experience, Lieutenant-General Sir Richard Butler, who had been at GHQ from 1915 into 1918, and Lieutenant-General Sir George Harper, promoted only ten days before from his beloved 51st Highland Division. The strains of fluid battle after years of long-prepared static operations were another matter.

The Allied Commanders: French Army

The French High Command revolved round three great contrasting figures: Pétain, the Commander-in-Chief; Général de Division Ferdinand Foch, the Chief of Staff; and Général de Division Marie Fayolle, the reserve army group commander. All were soon to be made marshals of France for vital

▲ The French Army's C-in-C since May 1917, Henri Pétain (1856-1951) was above all determined to preserve France's manpower from further losses. In line with his pre-war motto 'Firepower kills' he sought to do this by greater reliance on machines and defence in depth.

▲ Ferdinand Foch (1851-1929) was the new Allied supreme commander (26 March 1918), who was to win a prolonged 1918 strategic duel with Ludendorff. His immediate contribution to halting Kaiserschlacht was in urging on French reserves and making the retention of Amiens an undisputed essential as the pivot of the British and French armies. Aged 66 in his year of destiny, he proved more durable and energetic than many younger commanders.

but differing contributions to Allied victory. Pétain had nursed a French army half infected by mutinies back to health in the autumn of 1917, launching effective but limited local offensives at Verdun and Malmaison (Aisne). For 1918 his strategy of 'victory at the smallest price' rested on the twin pillars of increased mechanization (tanks, motorized heavy guns, aircraft, more infantry automatic weapons) and waiting for the American divisions to replace France's over-extended and expended manpower.

Foch, as Chief of Staff in Paris, had a broader outlook reinforced by a lengthy visit to the Italian Front. He remained convinced that only offensive action could win the war, and for this he needed a general Allied reserve of 20-30 divisions, troops that Haig and Pétain were reluctant to give him.

Fayolle, a white-haired professorial-looking gunner general plucked from retirement in 1914, is the least known to English-language readers. Yet he was already France's most dependable field commander, now emerged from the shadow of Pétain as the 'Saviour of Verdun's replacement in corps and army group commands. He had fought alongside the British on the Somme as Sixth Army commander, and had offered to resign in disappointment at gains that surpassed Haig's. Both his dispatch to Italy and recall in mid-February marked him out as the French Army's senior 'fire brigade' general. Pétain selected him for a revived reserve army group command, not unaware that Foch and political circles saw Fayolle as his replacement.

Two army commanders were designated to control Fayolle's divisions sent to Haig's help if Ludendorff attacked the British sector. Général de Division Georges Humbert was the longest serving French Army commander, familiar with the sector of which the British Fifth Army had recently relieved him, and before that 1914 commander of the élite Moroccan Division. Farther east, Général de Division Marie Debeney, Pétain's former 1917 Chief of Staff, commanded First Army east of Toul, earmarked to transfer six divisions to the Somme. He had not served with the British before, but Pétain's current chief of staff, Général de Division François Anthoine, had done so, alongside Gough, with success at Third Ypres.

1 *Général Marie Fayolle (1852-1928), France's reserve army group commander, was a courteous leader who won affection from subordinates and allies. He had been a schoolmate of Foch at the same Jesuit College and, more firmly than Pétain, wanted to keep the French Army connected to the British.*

2 *Général Georges Humbert (1862-1921), commander of the reserve French Third Army, was a veteran of France's pre-war colonial campaigns, most notably in Morocco 1913-14. From command of the crack Moroccan Division at the Marne, he rapidly rose to army command (July 1915). Like* other French generals in March 1918, he needed several days to get into his stride.

3 *The second French army commander to be engaged was Général Marie Debeney (1864-1937), of First Army. He had commanded 25th Division at Verdun and XXXII Corps in the 1916 Somme campaign. Prior to the battle he had urged Clemenceau to secure a single Allied command. Debeney reconnoitred his sector on 25 March, urged on by refugees, and the next evening Foch visited his headquarters to reinforce an already telephoned order to relieve the British XVIII Corps.*

THE OPPOSING ARMIES

The Western Front armies of 1918 were closer to those of the 1939-42 Blitzkrieg era than to their immediate 1914 forbears. Many factors reflect this. Soldiers were predominately recent conscripts rather than long-service regulars. The officers were mostly young, wartime commissioned and technically qualified as well as trench-hardened rather than scions of hereditary military families.

Organizationally, the familiar pattern of army groups down to 'triangular' nine-battalion divisions predominated, a process that had begun in 1915. The lowest unit level of squad/section consisted of riflemen escorting a light machine-gun team. Firepower was approaching an early Second World War scale. French and German divisions had an organic group/battalion of heavy guns (155mm/150mm calibre), and a German division had nearly as many mortars as its 1939 successor (which actually had more horses than its slimmer 1918 predecessor). Rifle grenades, mortars and flamethrowers had been infantry weapons since 1915.

Both sides relied considerably on motor transport especially for ambulances, and heavy-gun tractors and there were many motorcycles, but these did not supplant the importance of horse-drawn vehicle and railways. For the first time both sides had modest tank forces, and the French armoured cars, in particular, were to flourish in the new, more mobile fighting ahead. In the third dimension, close air support, already a feature of 1916-17 local fighting, was to become the norm on a much more massive and sustained scale that anticipated the tactical air forces of 1939-45.

Communications relied on large, cumbersome radios (at brigade level and higher), telephones, flares, lamps, visual signalling strips, aircraft-dropped messages, runners, and the motorized or mounted messenger. No method could guarantee prompt received reports in fluid action, nor would that be possible until the Allied introduction of the 'walkie talkie' in 1943.

German Forces

The most striking changes to the German Army in the West during the winter of 1917/18 were those of size and training. From being an outnumbered, defensive, trench-holding organization it became a superior army reinforced by 42 picked victorious divisions from the Eastern and Italian Fronts (4 divisions). Ludendorff concentrated 74 divisions for 'Michael'. No fewer than seven were Guard formations (two newly formed in January), three were Bavarian regular divisions and one was a Marine division from Flanders. Only thirteen divisions were reserve or Landwehr type, while as many as 20 were regular line formations of pre-1914 origin, nine of which had one or more élite grenadier regiments. No fewer than 18 divisions lining up for Kaiserschlacht had fought in the recent Riga, Caporetto and Cambrai operations.

Owing to the extensive transfer of individual soldiers over 35 years of age, the recall of wounded

15

ORDER OF BATTLE
GERMAN ARMY ON THE WESTERN FRONT, 21 MARCH 1918

192 Divisions, 110 in line, 82 in reserve, 136,618 officers, 3,438,288 men (1,232,000 rifles & 24,000 sabres), 764,563 horses, 13,832 guns, 8,845 mortars, 59,361 MGs and 3,668 front-line aircraft

Supreme Commander Kaiser Wilhelm II of Germany
Chief of General Staff Feldmarschall Hindenburg
First Quartermaster General Gen Ludendorff

468 miles OHL - Head of Operations Oberstleutnant Wetzell (HQ Avesnes)

KAISERSCHLACHT
50 miles
74 divisions, 6,608 guns, 3,534 mortars

ARMY GROUP RUPPRECHT
CoS Gen Kühl

ARMY GROUP CROWN PRINCE
CoS Oberst Schulenberg

ARMY GROUP GALLWITZ

ARMY GROUP ALBRECHT

Fourth Army	Sixth Army	Seventh Army	First Army	Third Army	Fifth Army	Army Det C
Arnim	Quast	Boehn	F Below	Einem	Gallwitz	Fuchs

KAISERSCHLACHT

Seventeenth Army
Below
(HQ St Armand)
18 divs, 2,236 guns

Second Army
Marwitz
(HQ Le Cateau)
20 divs, 1,789 guns

Eighteenth Army
Hutier
(HQ Guise)
27 divs, 2,448 guns, 9 tanks

Nineteenth Army
Bothmer

Army Dets A & B
Mudra & Gündell

Reserves of 9 or 11 divs
730 aircraft (82 sqns)

Note: German average divisional strength in 1918: 12,300 men; 6-12 lorries; about 3,000 horses; 48 field and heavy guns; 120 mortars; 78 MG08 and 144 Bergmann LMGs

ORDER OF BATTLE
GERMAN SEVENTEENTH ARMY

Gen der Inf Otto von Below
2,234 guns (824 heavy), 1,197 mortars, 241 serviceable aircraft (380 total)

Chef der Genst Genlt Krafft von Dellmensingen

XVIII Corps	VI Res Corps	XIV Res Corps	XI Corps
GenIt Albrecht	GenIt von dem Borne	GenIt von Lindequist	GenIt Kühne
111th, 221st, 234th Divs	17th, 195th Divs	3rd Gd, 20th Divs	24th Res, 53rd Res Divs
2nd Gd Res Div	1st Gd Res, 5th Bav Div	39th Div	119th Div
239th Div	24th Div		4th Div

▲ *German infantry practice in February 1918 for the renewal of open warfare. They are advancing in platoon or squad files. In the centre foreground is a light machine-gun gruppe with the model 08/15 gun (introduced December 1916). Each company had at least four such weapons by January 1918. (IWM Q29948)*

and rear area personnel, the ranks were full of younger, experienced men to such an extent that one-third to half an infantry platoon may have contained troops trained before the war. On the other hand the ranks included the 1919 conscript class and even 16-year-olds; the younger, fitter men especially composed the famous *Stosstruppen*, which had been formed since 1916. These were special units of unmarried men under 25 on double rations who were assigned to trench attacks and raiding, most 'attack' divisions getting a 120-man assault company split by platoons between the three line regiments. By 1918 each Western Front Army on paper had a training *Sturmbataillone* with four companies, a machine-gun company plus flamethrower, mortar and 37mm infantry gun detachments. Below's Seventeenth Army's *Sturmbataillone* was the 8th, but Hutier's known allotment was only a company, the 18th. Marwitz's Second Army had the 3rd Jäger Assault Battalion of Caporetto and Cambrai veterans. It is im-

possible to know how many actual specialized stormtroops attacked on 21 March. Adding up the entire known 1918 Western Front Army-level unit listing yields only ten battalions and five companies, or perhaps 6,600 troops. Giving each of the 32 first-line attack divisions a company takes the combined total to about 10,000.

What is clear is that most Kaiserschlacht forces, 56 divisions or about 800,000 men, underwent three weeks of comprehensive day and night war-of-movement tactical training, often with stormtroop instructors and with live ammunition. The 111th Division, for example, twice practised its full-scale breakthrough on a marked out trench system. Some divisions trained in Russia and Roumania, even before their transfer to the West. Training emphasized company/platoon commander leadership, a return to rifle marksmanship, mastery of the Bergmann light machine-gun and trench grenading. It also entailed long approach marches, up to 27½ miles a day.

Such was the confidence engendered that soldiers talked of the 'Hindenburg flat race'; the vital thing was to keep up with the Feuerwalz creeping artillery barrage, paced at 300 metres every four minutes. Ironically, cavalry represented this on exercise with their lances – a rather more prominent role than they would play in the actual

A7V Sturmpanzerwagen (1918)

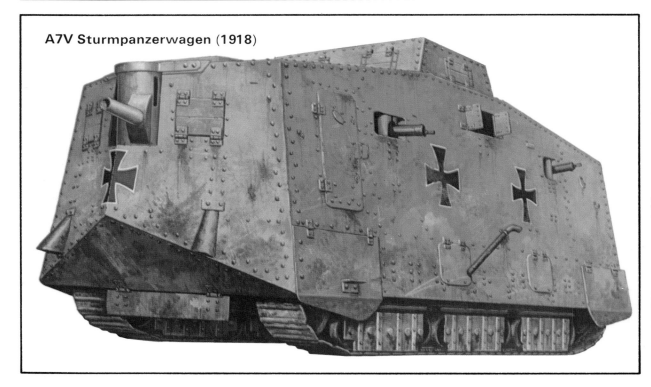

▲*Only ten examples of Germany's first tank, the A7V Sturmpanzerwagen, were ready for Kaiserschlacht. Four of a section of five were actually used on the first day, manned and supported by 176 all ranks (81 drivers and 70 gunners), in the first of the nine 1918 German tank attacks. Two officers and* *sixteen men manned the A7V's 240sq ft fighting compartment, beginning with a 57mm (ex-Russian) Sokol gun in the bow and six 7.92mm MG08 Maxim-type guns round the other sides. Designed by Josef Vollmer, the A7V was named after the presiding Allgemeine-Kriegs-Department, 7 Abteilung Verkehrswesen* *(Traffic Section) Committee. Twin 4-cylinder Daimler-Benz engines drove its 33-ton box bulk at 8mph on the flat with Holt-tractor suspension, which was sprung however. Its 26¼ft long, 10ft wide and 11ft high body was clad in 15-30mm solid-sheet armour, but had only 1½in ground clearance.* *Kaiserschlacht's first day would not reveal its shortcomings. Four A7Vs supported XVII Corps south of St. Quentin, helping 36th (West Prussia) Division capture the 12th Irish Rifles' Le Pontchu redoubt south of the third trench from the old front-line system by 3.15 p.m.*

fighting. Significantly, that barrage could only be speeded up, not slowed or lifted, by the storm-troops' green rocket flares. Attention to detail included maps sewn on to their cuffs and photographs of BEF defences issued to companies. Every infantry company also had a bugler capable of sounding 24 different calls and thus able to act as substitute means of communication in the advance before telephone lines were brought forward.

The guiding genius of Ludendorff's artillery 'battering train' was Oberst Georg 'Durchbruch' ('Breakthrough') Bruchmüller, a pre-war retired officer, who had perfected a successful technique

of brief gas-shell-laced drumfire bombardments in the less demanding conditions of the Eastern Front, most recently at Riga. He had been on the Western Front since the Cambrai counter-attack. Bruchmüller's technique had three general phases: first, surprise fire, without registering batteries, to the full depth of the enemy's position, including much gas shell of different kinds; second, a general counter-battery phase to silence or at least temporarily blind the defending guns; and, third, fire on specific targets, especially forward trenches.

In relation to this Feuerwalz, Bruchmüller later revealingly wrote: 'The thanks of the infantry

ORDER OF BATTLE
GERMAN SECOND ARMY

Gen der Kav Georg von der Marwitz
1,751 guns (714 heavy), 1,080 mortars, 232 serviceable aircraft (340 total)

Chef der Genst Oberst von Tschischwitz

XXXIX Res Corps
Gen der Inf von Stäbs

16th Res, 21st Res Divs

XXIII Res Corps
Gen der Inf von Kathen

18th Div, 50th Res, 79th Res Divs
9th Res Div
13th, 199th Divs

LI Corps
Gen von Hofacker

208th Div
19th Div
Gd Ersatz Div

XIII Corps
Gen der Inf von Watter

27th, 107th, 183rd Divs
54th Res Div
3rd Marine Div

XIV Corps
Genlt von Gontard

4th Gd, 25th Divs
1st Div
228th Div

ORDER OF BATTLE
GERMAN EIGHTEENTH ARMY

Gen der Inf Oskar von Hutier
2,623 guns (970 heavy), 1,257 mortars, 9 tanks, 257 serviceable aircraft (350 total)

Chef der Genst Genmjr von Sauberzweig

Genlt von Lüttwitz

28th, 88th, 113th Divs
5th, 6th, 206th Divs
23rd Div

XVII Corps
Genlt von Werern

1st Bav, 36th, 238th Divs
9th, 10th Divs
7th Res, 10th Res Divs
(4 A7V tanks)

Gruppe Gayl
Gen der Inf von Gayl

14th Landwehr, 47th Res Divs
223rd Div
211th Div

IX Corps
Genlt von Oetinger

45th Res, 50th Divs
5th Gd, 231st Divs
1st Gd Div
(5 Mk IV tanks)

IV Res Corps
Genlt von Conta

34th, 37th, 103rd Divs
33rd Div

OHL Reserve

2nd Gd, 26th & 12th Divs

◄ *A German 76mm light trench mortar battery practises advancing across snow-covered ground. The 76mm mortars are mule-drawn. Each 1918 battalion had four of these weapons. (IWM Q29969)*

▶ *A German Eighteenth Army 77mm field gun team advancing near Rancourt, south-east of St. Quentin, in February 1918. This was the German Army's standard field piece, 2,514 equipping the three Kaiserschlacht armies, 24 (two battalions with six four-gun batteries) per division with additional non-organic battalions. The gun fired a 15lb shell to 7,500 yards. (IWM Q29884)*

◄ *German 76mm light trench mortars being manhandled over shelled ground on the Western Front, February 1918. One of the crew is carrying a large traversing handspike. These accurate, rifled weapons were an essential element of Kaiserschlacht. They fired for the first 20 and the last five minutes of the bombardment, then contributed to the creeping barrage. (IWM Q29888)*

◄ *German artillerymen manhandle forward a Model 1913 130mm heavy field gun, probably in the Somme region. The gun weighed 5.7 tons and fired an 89lb shell to a range of nearly 15,750 yards (9 miles). Rate of fire was two rounds a minute and maximum elevation 26°. Seventeenth and Second Armies had 39 of these pieces organized in two-gun batteries. (IWM Q56559)*

... must be treasured more by every artillery man than all orders and citations.' His preparations required nearly half the total artillery on the Western Front. To register so many new guns without betraying their presence by shooting was the work of Captain Pulkowsky. He used a variant of the British pre-Cambrai calibration solution: i.e., test firing a gun to obtain its ballistics and matching this with meteorological and map data. About 6,000 officers and NCOs were so instructed by him before 21 March. Even so this pre-registration was only fully achieved in Bruchmüller's own Eighteenth Army sector; the other two Armies' guns did take ranging shots.

Some batteries returned to Germany for re-equipping with new guns so as to have new, unworn barrels that would not drop shells short. The 1,000 or so guns moved from the Eastern Front were calibrated on one huge firing range. The scale of Kaiserschlacht's artillery preparation was also concealed by a night delivery of camouflaged ammunition dumps that began only eleven days before 'Der Tag'. The concealed guns only began moving a week before and the final units the night before into pre-marked positions.

Ludendorff did not neglect morale. Some Prussian soldiers (i.e., not Bavarian, Saxon or Württemberger) were told the war would be over in three months. Patriotic instruction was given over the winter by carefully selected officers. Much home leave was granted. Decorations were lavishly distributed, notably on the Kaiser's birthday. Military bands gave frequent concerts and accompanied the singing troops on their final concentration marches. Some troops looked forward to the ample food and drink known to be in the BEF's hands. Indeed, the general conviction was planted, despite all the horrors of *Stellungskrieg*, that with Russia out of the war, peace could come only through one last victorious German offensive.

The German Air Force

German Air Force winter preparations were on a similar scale, beginning with a staff wargame and intensifying with photographic missions from mid-January. The most significant aspect was multiplied emphasis on ground attack, which was symbolized by the March 1918 renaming of *Schutzstaffeln* ('protection squadrons') as *Schlachtstaffeln* ('battle squadrons'); eight such units flew from the East to join 30 already in the West. The Army's manual *The Attack in Positional Warfare* devoted a whole section to air support, which was reinforced by a document of 20 February, *Employ-*

◄ Rows of German poison-gas projectors are deployed on the Western Front, February 1918. The Pioneer Corps provided the personnel for gas warfare regiments. Gas artillery shells were now the major means of delivering lethal agents, but projectors were also used from December 1917. The projectors were retooled out-of-date 180mm mortars, able to fire three or four gallons of agent, usually phosgene (Green Cross), a mile or two when elevated to about 45°. On 21 March projectors were used ineffectually against the British XVII Corps north of the River Scarpe. (IWM Q48449)

◀ *German Hannover CL (Light C Category) II ground-attack two-seater of Schlachtstaffel 12. The type appeared in 1917. Its 180hp Argus As III in-line engine gave a top speed of 103mph at sea level and a 24,600ft ceiling. Rate of climb was 5 minutes 18 seconds to 3,280ft, and endurance 3 hours. Armament was a ring-mounted 7.92mm drum-fed Parabellum Model 14 for the observer, whose field of fire was increased by the small biplane tail, with one or two synchronized 7.92mm Spandau machine-guns firing forward. Stick grenades or fragmentation bombs were carried in racks either side of the observer's position. The Hannover's plywood covered fuselage could sustain damage, and low-altitude agility was good.*

▼ *A German artillery observation AE balloon with its ground crew (normally 24 men) and winding wagon among the cratered fields, photographed by an Infanterieflieger from about 164 feet. Prior to the offensive each balloon platoon was given a reserve balloon and a week's supply of gas (instead of two days' previously). The AE could climb to 1,500 metres with two observers and operate in 50mph winds. German balloons not only spotted on 21 March but also subsequently, including for the Somme crossings on the 25th. Their nineteen British opponents were soon returned to depot and their crews used as Lewis gunners or to dig defences.*

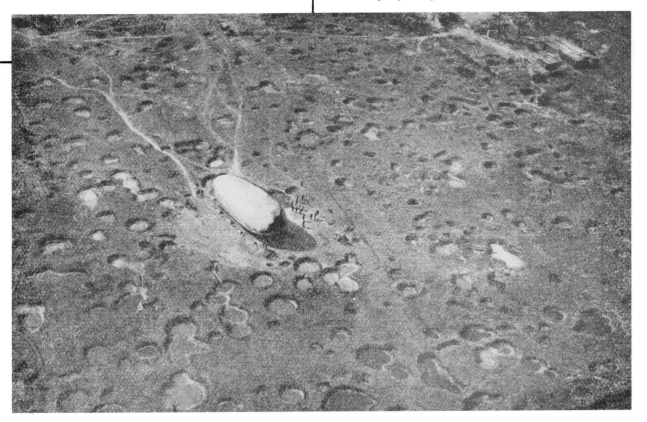

ment of Battle Flights stressing their use under divisional command at the very moment the infantry went over the top. This was in slight contrast to the successful use of at least 30 low-flying *Schutzstaffeln* aircraft at Cambrai immediately before and during the ground counter-attack.

Two new fighter Jagdgeschwadern joined Manfred von Richthofen's famous formation. These three commands controlled twelve of the 35 *Staffeln* (326 fighters) allocated to 'Michael' or nearly 45 per cent of Germany's total fighter strength. Nearly a third of artillery cooperation and over half of the available bomber units were concentrated to support the three Kaiserschlacht armies. Flying in only took place on 9-12 March, with flights over new airfields only allowed from the 17th. The Air Force's contribution also included 45 observation balloons with a week's gas supply and several hundred anti-aircraft guns (of 1,137 on the Western Front on 21 March) all given improved mobility.

The British Expeditionary Force

Haig's armies were depleted and to some extent disheartened formations in the spring of 1918. That depletion was most marked in the infantry whose effective strength on 1 March of 514,637 was only 36 per cent of total strength as compared with 45 per cent only six months earlier. As a result, the BEF was forced to abandon its twelve battalions per division for the Franco-German standard of nine. In the process no fewer than 141 wartime-raised units disappeared between 10 January and 4 March, for the War Office decreed that only battalions of Kitchener's New Army volunteer or 2nd Line Territorial origin should be abolished. This blow, affecting 47 divisions, was cushioned to the extent that 38 battalions amalgamated to make 19 and that all disbanded units were absorbed into a sister battalion of the same regiment (though not necessarily within the same division).

This efficiently executed contraction at least ensured that average battalion strength on 21 March was a substantial 995 all ranks. It may have afforded some wry consolation to the British line

infantry with new hybrid loyalties that even the élite Guards Division had to yield a brigade to stiffen the prosaic north country 31st (New Army) Division. Likewise a Highland brigade replaced 61st Division's disbanded battalions. Significantly, and despite their much longer overseas reinforcement process, the ten Dominion (Australian, New Zealand and Canadian) divisions retained their old twelve-battalion quadrilateral structure.

Another portent of 1918's thinner ranks but greater firepower was that before 21 March most divisions received an additional company of sixteen Vickers heavy machine-guns, making a total of 64. All infantry battalions had double the 1917 allocation of 16 Lewis guns. Fifth Army's slender manpower was further bolstered by more tanks, aircraft and far more artillery than Third Army. Gough received no fewer than 23 Army field artillery brigades, but even this only gave him one field gun or howitzer for every 70 yards of his extended sector.

The BEF reorganization reduced the already short time available for training and working on defences. The latter task was not helped when each division's all-purpose pioneer battalion shrank from four companies to three. Defence in depth was a difficult concept to teach troops who had not generally fought on the defensive since May 1915. Nevertheless staffs at least carried out counter-attack terrain reconnaissance; in Third Army the whole of 25th Division rehearsed this.

If the morale of 'Bing's Boys' was higher than that of Gough's reassembled, much tried Fifth Army, the BEF as a whole benefited from more generous leave, 88,000 on the eve of 21 March. Up to 17 per cent of a division's infantry might be on leave at anyone time. GHQ counted only 1,921 absentees without leave from the entire BEF in March 1918. Martin Middlebrook is probably correct in adducing a recovery in morale from the turn of the year's post-Passchendaele depths.

The Royal Flying Corps (RFC) faced a completely new heightened identity as the Royal Air Force before Kaiserschlacht ran its course. In France, Major-General Sir John Salmond commanded 31,092 other ranks and 1,255 operational aircraft. Early in March he reinforced Fifth Army with six extra squadrons (114 aircraft).

ORDER OF BATTLE
ALLIED ARMIES ON THE WESTERN FRONT,
SPRING 1918

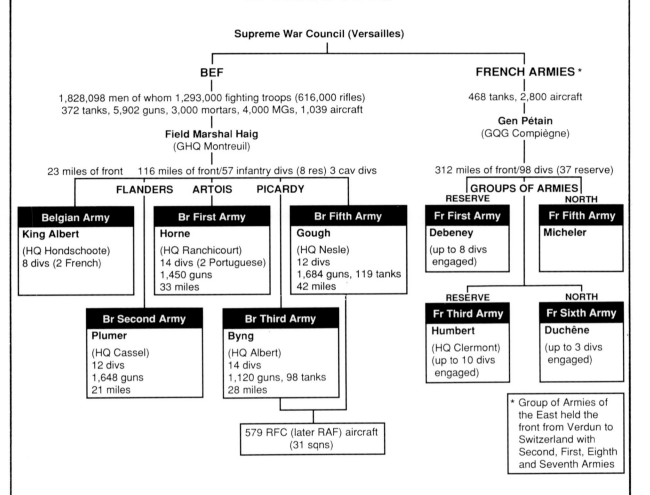

Supreme War Council (Versailles)

BEF

1,828,098 men of whom 1,293,000 fighting troops (616,000 rifles)
372 tanks, 5,902 guns, 3,000 mortars, 4,000 MGs, 1,039 aircraft

Field Marshal Haig
(GHQ Montreuil)

23 miles of front   116 miles of front/57 infantry divs (8 res) 3 cav divs

FLANDERS   ARTOIS   PICARDY

Belgian Army

King Albert

(HQ Hondschoote)
8 divs (2 French)

Br First Army

Horne

(HQ Ranchicourt)
14 divs (2 Portuguese)
1,450 guns
33 miles

Br Fifth Army

Gough

(HQ Nesle)
12 divs
1,684 guns, 119 tanks
42 miles

Br Second Army

Plumer

(HQ Cassel)
12 divs
1,648 guns
21 miles

Br Third Army

Byng

(HQ Albert)
14 divs
1,120 guns, 98 tanks
28 miles

579 RFC (later RAF) aircraft
(31 sqns)

FRENCH ARMIES *

468 tanks, 2,800 aircraft

Gen Pétain
(GQG Compiègne)

312 miles of front/98 divs (37 reserve)

GROUPS OF ARMIES
RESERVE   NORTH

Fr First Army

Debeney

(up to 8 divs
engaged)

Fr Fifth Army

Micheler

RESERVE   NORTH

Fr Third Army

Humbert

(HQ Clermont)
(up to 10 divs
engaged)

Fr Sixth Army

Duchêne

(up to 3 divs
engaged)

* Group of Armies of
the East held the
front from Verdun to
Switzerland with
Second, First, Eighth
and Seventh Armies

Note: British average divisional strength in 1918:
11,800 men (13,035 establishment; 3,673 horses
and mules; 768 carts and wagons; 358 bicycles
and motorcycles; 14 lorries and cars; 21 motor
ambulances; 48 field guns; 36 mortars; 64 Vickers
MGs; 144+ Lewis MGs).

French divisions averaged 11,400 men; 48 field
and heavy guns; 18 mortars; 9 infantry 37mm guns;
108 MGs; 216 LMGs.

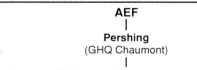

AEF

Pershing
(GHQ Chaumont)

254,378 men in Europe of whom 162,482 combat troops
Four 28,000-strong combat divisions formed,
units holding 17 miles of front by 20 March

ORDER OF BATTLE
BRITISH THIRD ARMY, 21 MARCH 1918

Gen the Hon Sir J Byng

CoS Maj-Gen L Vaughan
CRA Maj-Gen R St C Lecky 1,120 guns (461 heavy)
CRE Maj-Gen W A Liddell
RFC Brig-Gen J F A Higgins (III Bde, 261 aircraft)

XVII Corps
Lt-Gen Sir C Fergusson

4th, 15th Divs
Gds Div
234 guns (103 heavy)
(5.25 mile front)

IV Corps
Lt-Gen Sir G Harper

6th, 51st Divs
25th Div
242 guns (98 heavy)
(7 mile front)

Army Troops

IV Tank Bde:
(3 bns, 98 tanks)
AA: 5 btys
Engineers:
54 coys & units

VI Corps
Lt-Gen Sir J Haldane

3rd, 34th, 59th Divs
324 guns (132 heavy)
(7.33 mile front)

V Corps
Lt-Gen Sir E Fanshawe

17th, 63rd, 47th Divs
2nd, 19th Divs
320 guns (128 heavy)
(8.5 mile front)

ORDER OF BATTLE
BRITISH FIFTH ARMY, 21 MARCH 1918

Gen Sir H Gough

CoS Maj-Gen J Percy
CRA Maj-Gen H C C Uniacke 1,784 guns (532 heavy)
CRE Maj-Gen P G Grant
RFC Brig-Gen L E O Charlton (V Bde, 357 aircraft)

VII Corps
Lt-Gen Sir W Congreve

9th, 21st, 16th Divs
39th Div (in GHQ reserve)
433 guns (150 heavy)
12 tanks
(7 mile front)

XVIII Corps
Lt-Gen Sir I Maxse

61st, 30th, 36th Divs
411 guns (129 heavy)
3rd Cav Div (under Army
command)
20th Div from 1pm, 21 March
(9 mile front)

Army Troops

(excuding artillery)
Cavalry: 6 regts
Tanks: IV Tank Bde
(3 bns, 119 tanks)
AA: 4 btys
Engineers: 56 coys & units
Signals & Pigeons:
24 sectns & units
Motor Transport: 6 coys
Inf & Mil Police: 2 coys &
1 sqdn
Medical: 39 units
Ordnance & Forestry:
5 units & 3 coys
Labour: 153 coys
Printing & Stationery:
1 sectn

XIX Corps
Lt-Gen Sir H Watts

66th, 24th Divs
1st Cav Div
366 guns (130 heavy)
50th Div from 3.20am, 21
March
(7 mile front)

III Corps
Lt-Gen Sir R Butler

14th, 18th, 58th Divs
2nd Cav Div
356 guns (106 heavy)
(19 mile front)

▶ *A private of 10th Battalion (1st Gwent) South Wales Borderers, 38th (Welsh) Division (New Army). He wears a vertical gold wound stripe, a long-service chevron, the Red Dragon of Wales divisional sign (upper left sleeve only) and a battalion symbol (red/black tower) on the green square indicating the third brigade. The 38th Division was transferred from First Army to V Corps (Third Army) on the night of 31 March/1 April but remained in reserve. The private has a pick on his back, No. 1 Mark II wire-cutter on his Lee-Enfield rifle muzzle, and an extra canvas ammunition bandolier over his leather winter jerkin.*

After Cambrai right up to 21 March, 24 officers from brigades, staffs and divisional artillery received four-day courses on air cooperation, including flying time. Disruptive bombing of German preparations began on 16 February and was intensified from 7 March.

The French Army

The state and morale of France's armies in the spring of 1918 are not easy to assess. British historians, taking their cue from Haig's dismissive 7 January opinion that the French could not withstand a sustained German offensive, are inclined to underestimate or ignore the French contribution in the Kaiserschlacht battle. The question mark arises from 1917's summer mutinies and how sensitive they still made the *poilu*. The last minor instances of indiscipline actually took place in late January 1918 – but it must be remembered that nearly half Pétain's divisions were never affected at all.

Ludendorff's operations chief, Oberstleutnant Georg Wetzell, assessed the French in December 1917 as 'rested and strategically free', 'better in the attack and more skilful in the defence, but are not such good stayers as the British'. In particular he evaluated their artillery as better than Haig's, and

British observers noted French reliance on their stronger artillery to defeat attacks. This was understandable when average divisional infantry strength was only 6,000.

Of the formations immediately earmarked to come to the BEF's help, 9th Division had six weeks of training and re-equipping for a war of movement. II Cavalry Corps was a picked force but one dissipated for a month beforehand by internal security duties in the strike-ridden south. French fears of a Russian-style civilian collapse were much greater than of a military one.

In firepower Pétain had two significant cards to play. First was the Réserve Générale d'Artillerie Française, organized by his gunner predecessor Général de Division Robert Nivelle and Général Edmond Buat, something like 1,000 lorry-borne 75s and 1,000 heavier tractor-drawn guns. On 1 March 1918, reserve stocks held 35 million field gun shells. Second, that same day Pétain approved formation of an analogous mobile Aviation Reserve for Northern Army Group. It consisted of two fighter and bomber *groupements* with up to 600 aircraft based at Soissons, Fère-en-Tardenois and Châlons-sur-Marne.

The French Army received its first Renault light tanks in March, but 'Le Char de la Victoire' would first see action only at the end of May.

◀ *Types of French infantry: from the left, a Fusilier-Mitrailleur with the 1915 Chauchat light machine-gun; Grenadier-Fusilier with rifle grenade; Voltigeur (ordinary rifleman); Grenadier-à-main with a bag of grenades; Rifleman in full assaulting order.*

OPPOSING PLANS

German Plans

The essence of Ludendorff's Operation 'Michael', as Kaiserschlacht was soon code-named by his planning staff, was that tactics dictated the strategy. The blow would be delivered at the earliest possible date but, once begun, the progress or otherwise of the attackers would dictate the exploitation.

'Michael' evolved over a period of four months. At the fateful Mons council of war (11 November 1917) Ludendorff himself was first to advocate an attack near St. Quentin to gain the Somme line, which could then be used as a protective flank against the French while the BEF was 'rolled up' by German advances to the north-west. Interestingly, the concept strongly prefigures that of May 1940, as did the then Oberst Hans von Seeckt's Western Front breakthrough scheme of March 1915, submitted to General der Infanterie Erich von Falkenhayn, Ludendorff's predecessor. There is no evidence Ludendorff knew of Seeckt's purely paper proposal, but it is striking that two of Imperial Germany's finest military brains were thinking on the same lines to achieve a Moltkian envelopment of the British. Ludendorff got his way against strong opposition from army group chiefs of staff who had been in the West for the duration. Generalleutnant von Kühl (Crown Prince Rupprecht's Group) wanted a Flanders thrust (later code-named 'George') towards Haze-brouck and the sea to cut off the BEF from the Channel ports and so anticipate Haig's expected 1918 Flanders offensive. Oberst von der Schulen-berg (German Crown Prince's Group), undaunted by 1916's concentrated slaughter, urged blows either side of Verdun ('Castor' and 'Pollux') to break France and pre-empt any Franco-American spring offensive. Somewhat surprisingly, he was supported by Ludendorff's able operations officer, Oberstleutnant Wetzell. The First Quartermaster General had no desire to emulate Falkenhayn at Verdun; in any case, Haig would probably attack in Flanders to relieve the French.

At the second Mons Conference (27 December) Ludendorff ordered preparation for five options: 'George' and its extension to the Ypres area; a 'Mars' drive at Arras; 'Michael' (St.

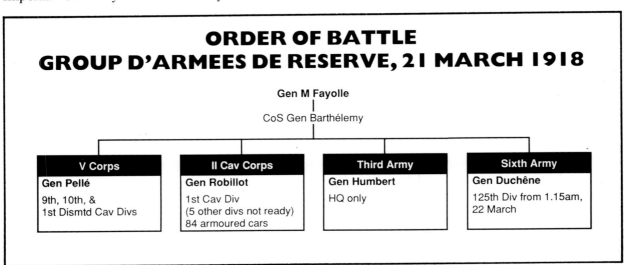

ORDER OF BATTLE
GROUP D'ARMEES DE RESERVE, 21 MARCH 1918

Gen M Fayolle

CoS Gen Barthélemy

V Corps	II Cav Corps	Third Army	Sixth Army
Gen Pellé	**Gen Robillot**	**Gen Humbert**	**Gen Duchêne**
9th, 10th, & 1st Dismtd Cav Divs	1st Cav Div (5 other divs not ready) 84 armoured cars	HQ only	125th Div from 1.15am, 22 March

Ludendorff's Western Front Offensives, 21 March to 1

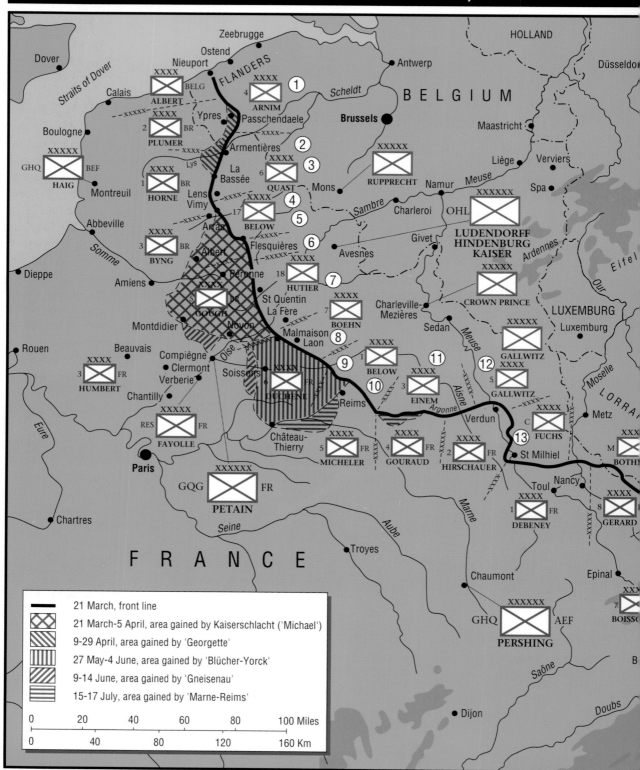

Legend:

- 21 March, front line
- 21 March–5 April, area gained by Kaiserschlacht ('Michael')
- 9–29 April, area gained by 'Georgette'
- 27 May–4 June, area gained by 'Blücher-Yorck'
- 9–14 June, area gained by 'Gneisenau'
- 15–17 July, area gained by 'Marne-Reims'

| 0 | 20 | 40 | 60 | 80 | 100 Miles |
| 0 | 40 | 80 | 120 | 160 Km |

July 1918

GERMAN
OFFENSIVE PLANS
1 George 2
2 George 1
3 Valkyrie
4 Mars
5 Michael 1
6 Michael 2
7 Michael 3
8 Archangel
9 Achilles
10 Roland
11 Hector
12 Castor
13 Pollux
14 Strassburg

◀ *Ludendorff's Western Front offensives 21 March to 17 July 1918. Alongside the opposing Allied and German armies on 21 March 1918 are shown the code-names for Ludendorff's offensive options. 'Michael' 1-3 and 'Mars' denote the extent of Kaiserschlacht, each being an Army's share. The ground won by Ludendorff's four lesser offensives after Kaiserschlacht is also shown.*

Quentin); and Verdun ('Castor' and 'Pollux'). The completion date was 10 March. On 21 January 1918, Ludendorff chose 'Michael' first after a lengthy tour of the front with Kühl and Schulenberg that included conferences with five army staffs. He judged 'George' too dependent on a dry spring and 'Mars' too dominated by the BEF-held Vimy Ridge. Three days later the orders went out.

'Michael' entailed three armies attacking on a record 50-mile front, three times Haig's 1916 Somme attack frontage. In the centre, Marwitz's Second Army would thrust for Péronne and encircle Byng's Cambrai salient from the south. To its north, Below's new Seventeenth Army would link up with Marwitz and advance on Bapaume. Hutier's Eighteenth Army would strike for Ham on the Somme. There it was to line the river against French intervention from the south while reinforcing the main offensive to the northwest on Arras and beyond. A third phase ultimately entailed rolling up the BEF from south (Arras) to north.

Very soon however Kaiserschlacht's purity of purpose was watered down. At the end of January, Hutier's new army passed to Army Group Crown Prince Wilhelm. Ludendorff wanted to exercise control via two army groups, not just through the Bavarian Rupprecht, who admired the British and wanted 'George' in Flanders more than 'Michael' in Picardy. But the Kaiser's son was responsible for the French sector of the front up to the Argonne. By the end of February he was pressing for a Hutier advance beyond the Somme and Crozat Canal. Ludendorff agreed, even to the extent of contemplating Eighteenth Army's reinforcement from the Crown Prince's three other armies, who were to withdraw into their battle zone if Pétain attacked them. Hutier's 15 March instruction to his five Corps Commanders specified reaching the line Chaulnes–Roye, up to 15 miles west of the Somme, in order to engage the French reserves.

Below's Seventeenth Army actually had the hardest task, for it had to punch below Byng's strong Arras bastion and then envelop it from the south in conjunction with its subsequent 'Mars' attack south of the Scarpe. Ominously, Below was refused permission to extend 'Mars' right up to that river. His army, the last formed, only equalled Hutier's in divisions and was weaker in guns and aircraft. Before it started Kaiserschlacht contained the seeds of strategic divergence.

German Tactics

Ludendorff was undoubtedly aware of the potential strategic contradictions but saw the tactical problem of breakthrough as paramount. As he told a doubting Rupprecht, 'We chop a hole, the rest follows. We did it that way in Russia.' It was at his bidding that Hauptmann Hermann Geyer wrote the battalion-and-above level *Der Angriff im Stellungskrieg* ('The Attack in Positional Warfare'), published on 26 January 1918, and widely distributed to the army. The core of this doctrine was infiltration, although no such German word was used. Ludendorff had ordered that every infantryman receive stormtrooper training. Small units of *Stosstruppen* or *Gruppen* were to advance continuously at speed and in depth past defending strongpoints that would be reduced by follow-up units of each division. The artillery creeping barrage was to keep up with the infantry attack rather than vice versa, and forward units would advance until they were exhausted instead of being relieved as in Allied methods. Each small unit was built round light machine-gunners and led by specially trained officers and NCOS. Follow-up battle groups had their own man-hauled *Minenwerfer*, and each regiment four horse-drawn field guns. Unusually these infantry regimental commanders commanded 150mm guns.

The minimum first-day objective was to advance about five miles to capture the British field gun line, and thereafter reserves were to reinforce success. Yet, crucially, Ludendorff had no arm of exploitation beyond his men's feet, the hooves of insufficient and underfed horses and motor transport often on iron tyres (owing to the rubber shortage). Nine tanks (including five Mk IVs captured from the British) were split between three corps, but when they reviewed them on 27 February these were the first tanks ever seen by Ludendorff or the Kaiser. Germany's first A7Vs (of 20 built) had been completed only in October 1917 so it was too late for a massive tank-building

programme (even if that had been favoured and had the raw materials been plentiful). Almost all the 32 Ehrhardt heavy armoured cars remained on the Eastern Front, especially in the Ukraine, as did captured Russian vehicles.

Cavalry existed only in the allocation of one squadron per division for scouting and escort duties; the three remaining cavalry divisions stayed in Russia. Even there their performance had been disappointing.

Allied Plans

By early December 1917, both Haig and Pétain realized and accepted they would have to fight defensively in the coming spring for the first time in the war. They were less happy about the details. Reluctantly, Haig relieved the French Third and Sixth Armies of 42 miles of front in Picardy down to and astride the River Oise by the end of January 1918. Both Allied C-in-Cs felt their armies to be understrength. Pétain disbanded three divisions in November-December 1917, and together the Allies lost eleven good divisions to prop up post-Caporetto Italy.

Ironically at this time of widening frontages and diminishing manpower, to which the American answer was still months away, the highest Allied deliberations focused on the need for a joint general reserve of up to 30 divisions to meet the expected German spring offensive, whether in Italy or France. The new Allied Supreme War Council wished to control this strategic force, an ambition reinforced when Foch became France's military representative early in February, and Lloyd George formally proposed its formation.

The scheme foundered on the lack of troops and the national C-in-Cs' equal reluctance to give up a significant number of divisions to the control of an international committee at Versailles. At dinner with Haig on 24 February, Clemenceau conceded that the Field Marshal and Pétain, rather than Foch, should agree on reserves. Next day Haig told the new CIGS, Wilson, that he would prefer to be relieved of command rather than release divisions. That and the imminence of Ludendorff's blow ended a complex but fruitless debate.

On the ground in the BEF zone, defence in depth was being dug according to the GHQ memorandum of 14 December 1917. This was not only based on German 1916-17 methods and manuals but actually urged the latter's study in translation. In theory these defences were to be up to 12 miles deep in three layers. The first was the Forward Zone of concealed machine-gun posts covering thick barbed-wire obstacles and other garrisoned all-round strongpoints or redoubts behind the front trench. These were to check the weight of German assault and force it to expend valuable time, manpower and ammunition. The main battle was to be fought and won in the Battle Zone a mile or two behind. This 2,000-3,000-yard deep area had larger wired-in redoubts and all the divisional artillery (apart from singly-placed anti-tank field guns in the Forward Zone). Each division had at least three battalions available to man the Battle Zone, with another outside in reserve for local counter-attack. Also close behind the Battle Zone were the heavy gun batteries. Last of all was the Rear Zone, a second battle zone in layout, four to eight miles behind the main zone of resistance. Behind its front Green Line lay headquarters, supply dumps and the heaviest guns – but its construction came third in the order of priorities.

Impressive on paper, this scheme was heavily handicapped by shortage of time and labour as well as hard January weather. In addition to troops, Gough had only a maximum of 8,830 labourers building defences. His Battle Zone on 21 March had no dugouts and was incomplete between St. Quentin and the Oise; and the Rear Zone consisted simply of a marked-out single trench, the 'Green Line'. Byng's defences were stronger, but his Battle Zone lacked machine-gun post dugouts, and the incomplete Rear Zone mustered three belts of wire, two waist-deep trench lines and machine-gun nests.

There was also the problem of accustoming the troops to these radical changes. The army commanders on 17 February lamented that their men did not understand the concept 'defence in depth'. One sadly anonymous regular NCO of 1914 commented 'It don't suit us. The British Army fights in line and won't do any good in these bird cages.' The Forward Zone was overmanned, compared with German or French 'outpost' methods, by troops insufficiently trained for their role but uneasily aware that it was sacrificial. The anti-tank 18-pounders and 60lb spherical trench-mortar shells adapted into anti-tank mines (plus wide ditches in the Battle Zone) may have given comfort against a feared Cambrai in reverse, but in fact it proved a sad waste of resources.

For the first time the British Tank Corps (10,072 men and 372 tanks in France), re-organizing and re-equipping, faced a defensive battle. New doctrine was only resolved early in March that they should be deployed in three groups up to ten miles behind the Front for corps or divisional Battle Zone counter-attacks rather than as single mobile 'Savage Rabbits' ambushing from concealed positions.

Fifth Army's vulnerability at least won Gough permission from GHQ in February to conduct a fighting withdrawal to the large Péronne bridge-head east of the Somme, on which 9,700 troops and labourers belatedly worked (10 March) behind the token Rear Zone. Gough would have preferred more reserve divisions for counter-attack, but three written appeals to GHQ failed to win more than three, two of which were located far behind his front-line while two were also under GHQ control. Worse, Haig's Chief of Staff forbade him to move them closer on the evening of 19th.

As early as 7 December 1917, BEF Intelligence had no difficulty in predicting a Ludendorff March offensive. Its precise sector was another matter. The RFC only found 500 tarpaulin-covered ammunition dumps in the St. Quentin area on 10-11 March. By 2 March, Brigadier-General Edgar Cox expected Third and Fifth Armies to face the onslaught, but his chief believed that it would extend along no more than 30-40 miles because of the amount of artillery, so the 17 March assessment emphasis was on Arras–St. Quentin, not south of the latter town. German security (for instance, no telephone traffic allowed within seven miles, of the Front, and camouflage, with night movements as late as possible) gave very little precise warning time. Gough, to his credit, took alarm in late January the moment he knew Hutier was his opponent.

BEF threat assessment and the crucial arrangements for French help were affected by Pétain's concern for his far longer front, which in turn was heightened by Ludendorff's diversions. These pleasantly included mustard gas shelling that caused 7,223 casualties from 9 March at points along the entire Western Front. There were fierce feint attacks on the Belgians, bombardments of Verdun, and in Lorraine on 20 March a German observation balloon fell in French lines with documents conveniently revealing an offensive for the 26th in Champagne (the 'Roland' option). None the less, on 7 March Haig and Pétain had agreed that six French divisions plus extra artillery and support units would concentrate in any of three areas north and south of Amiens by the fourth evening of a major offensive against the BEF. From the Montdidier–Noyon area they might secure Somme bridgeheads, hold Fifth Army's zone, and/or counter-attack. Four infantry and two cavalry divisions were deployed so as to be available, but nearly half Pétain's 39 reserve divisions were east of the Argonne.

French Intelligence meanwhile worked on Ludendorff's ultra-secure five-letter field cipher, which had been introduced for Kaiserschlacht on 5 March. By about 4 April it would be solved. This would influence later 1918 battles but not Kaiserschlacht itself.

▼*A German heavy rail gun, probably of 280mm (11in) calibre, fires from Le Cateau Wood, southeast of Cambrai. Eight of these guns took part in the opening bombardment.* *They could fire a 529lb shell 18 miles. (IWM Q29970)*

KAISERSCHLACHT 1918: THE BATTLE

The German Bombardment

At around 4.40 a.m. on 21 March 1918 a large white rocket soared above St. Quentin. It was the signal for 10,000 German gun and mortar crews to open fire simultaneously in a 43-mile wide bombardment covering 150 square miles, a barrage on a scale that would be surpassed only by the Red Army's 1945 attack on Berlin. In five hours, Ludendorff's 'Battering Train' expended 1,160,000 shells – Haig's guns had fired 1,732,873 shells *in a week* for the 1916 Somme attack. Every piece used 200-600 rounds. There are many vivid descriptions of the shelling elsewhere, so here we set out the seven phases planned by Oberst Bruchmüller, who was not, it should be pointed out, overall artillery chief (there was none) but only Eighteenth Army's.

Phase 1 4.40-6.40 a.m. 'General surprise fire' with gas and high-explosive (4:1 proportion) on all targets. 5.00 a.m. Trench mortars cease-fire. 5.30-40 a.m. Surprise fire on infantry positions by all guns below 170mm calibre; HE only against Forward Zone; HE and gas on Battle Zone. 6.00 a.m. Sunrise.

Phases 2-4: 6.40-7.10 a.m. Each 10 minutes including infantry gun ranging thwarted by fog.

Phase 5: 7.10-8.20 a.m. 70 minutes' fire by most batteries on infantry defences; counter- and long-range batteries shelling usual targets. 7.40-7.55 a.m. Some howitzers sweeping Forward Zone trenches; others shelling centres of resistance for 10 minutes and sweeping backwards. (Fog caused firing by map from here on.) Field guns sweeping between British 2nd line and intermediate positions with tear-gas shell and HE.

Phase 6: 8.20-9.35 a.m. Same as Phase 5 with target variations. Some smoke-shell to enhance fog.

Phase 7: 9.35-9.40 Howitzers shelling forward trenches with HE, with mortars and field guns firing on Forward Zone beyond.

Dislocation and paralysis were Bruchmüller's achieved aims. The Royal Artillery's replying 2,500 gun teams had to wear gas masks and its observers could not see SOS flares from Forward Zone redoubts. Specific targets hit included Fifth Army's railhead; airfields; Bapaume; Péronne; Flesquières salient (3,000 mustard gas casualties); three tank battalions' petrol and ammunition (destroyed). Some 7,500-8,000 troops were killed or wounded; 6ft-underground telephone lines were severed throughout the Forward and Battle Zones; and the latter's 70-80 infantry battalions took losses as they manned the defences. The maelstrom was not confined to the 'Michael' sector; it extended to the BEF's First and Second Armies as well as to the French in Champagne.

21 March: Infantry Assault

The first stormtroops and pioneers began cutting British wire from about 9 a.m. Forty minutes later the assault infantry of Ludendorff's 32 first-wave divisions advanced without cheers and in gas masks behind the creeping barrage 300 yards ahead from their close-support 77mm and 105mm batteries, light mortars and 150mm howitzers. In the lead were the army-level and divisional stormtroops, in company units with heavy weapons. They scrambled through the thick fog of the Forward Zone often to reach its redoubts or even those of the Battle Zone in 20-30 minutes. The second assault wave of infantry regiments followed only 100 yards behind, tasked to reduce these strongpoints from behind or from the flanks.

By 11.10 a.m., after 90 minutes' infantry fighting, only fifteen British Forward Zone redoubts still held out. The fog had ensured that a hundred 18-pounders and countless machine-guns were overrun without firing a shot and that 47 battalions, or perhaps 28,000 troops, had disappeared from the BEF order of battle. One battalion was a total loss; at least four other units had fewer than 50 survivors. Four of the eighteen divisions holding the line were to lose more than 2,000 men captured, mostly troops surrendering in positions cut-off and surrounded by overwhelming numbers. These were men who had already been through an unimaginable ordeal of five hours' shelling on a chemical battlefield in visibility at its worst. Many dazed captives were sent back through German lines unescorted.

The struggle for the British Battle Zone was simultaneous with that for the Forward Zone for over an hour of the morning, but the German need to wait for the prearranged creeping barrage did give the defence some respite, based as it was on the main gun line of each division. Three of Below's divisions thrust along the natural approach of the Hirondelle Valley right at the junction of Byng's IV and VI Corps and eventually destroyed four of 59th Divisions's battalions, capturing 36 of its 48 guns but not before one 4.5in howitzer had

fired about a thousand shells. In this sector Byng was falsely informed of Bullecourt's fall around noon only to discover the truth two hours later. The 6th and 51st Divisions were also driven back to the rear of the Battle Zone. V Corps in the Flesquières salient, heavily gassed but not directly attacked, was ordered by him that evening to withdraw 4,000 yards to an intermediate line.

Yet the salient was not cut off as Ludendorff planned, in the south thanks to staunch resistance by Gough's two northernmost divisions which held Epehy and well forward in the Battle Zone. Their tired neighbour, 16th (Irish) Division, succumbed after three counter-attacks to about a dozen of Marwitz's divisions, which destroyed two of the Irish brigades and captured 86 of 96 field pieces. Gough directed his reserve 39th Division to this

▼*A German gunner cools a hot gun barrel with wet rags. The piece is a 100mm field gun and is at near full 30° elevation. The Model 1917 fired a 39.5lb shell 12,085 yards (6.8 miles) at two rounds a minute. This is one of 530 such guns used on 21 March; they included eight Austro-Hungarian pieces. (IWM Q56535)*

sector and a dangerous gap was plugged with the aid of point-blank fire by three 9.2in howitzers. The far-off 50th Division began marching for the Somme bridges to aid Lieutenant-General Sir Herbert Watts' hard-hit XIX Corps, which had been forced to the rear of its Battle Zone. In the centre of Fifth Army, Lieutenant-General Sir Ivor Maxse's XVIII Corps held six miles of its Battle Zone all day against 14 of Hutier's divisions despite receiving only 50 survivors from the eight battalions in the Forward Zone, where six of the fourteen redoubts held out for at least five hours.

Butler's III Corps, the farthest south and the most extended, had only about 10,000 infantry for a 10-mile sector against which Hutier concentrated ten divisions with Germany's first armour. By 11 a.m. about fifteen battalions were advancing

into 14th Division's Battle Zone, having broken through on the boundary with 36th Ulster Division and to the south. By 2 p.m., 14th Division was on the rear of its Battle Zone and three-and-a-half hours' fighting later was forced from it. For a time the defenders were severed from an artillery-sustained 18th Division to the south, until 5th Dismounted Brigade restored the line for nightfall.

Around 2 p.m. Gough telephoned momentously to all his five corps commanders, telling them they must fight a delaying action until Allied reinforcements arrived and not be destroyed in the Battle Zone. In particular he gave Butler, who lamented the loss of many guns (actually 100), the prearranged permission to withdraw behind the Crozat Canal that night. He then visited all five subordinates in turn by car within three hours.

One brighter feature for Byng was an evening counter-attack by twelve tanks and about 400 infantry of 19th Division that retook most of Doignies village on the north flank of the Flesquières salient.

Martin Middlebrook, the first day's meticulous historian, has compiled its massive balance sheet.

▼ *The first batch of British prisoners of war march through a village south of St. Quentin on 21 March. Many of these Fifth Army infantry and gunners understandably* *seem to be relieved to be out of the war. The German Eighteenth Army modestly claimed 7,000 prisoners and 88 guns on the first day. (IWM Q51460)*

Opposing Forces, 21 March 1918

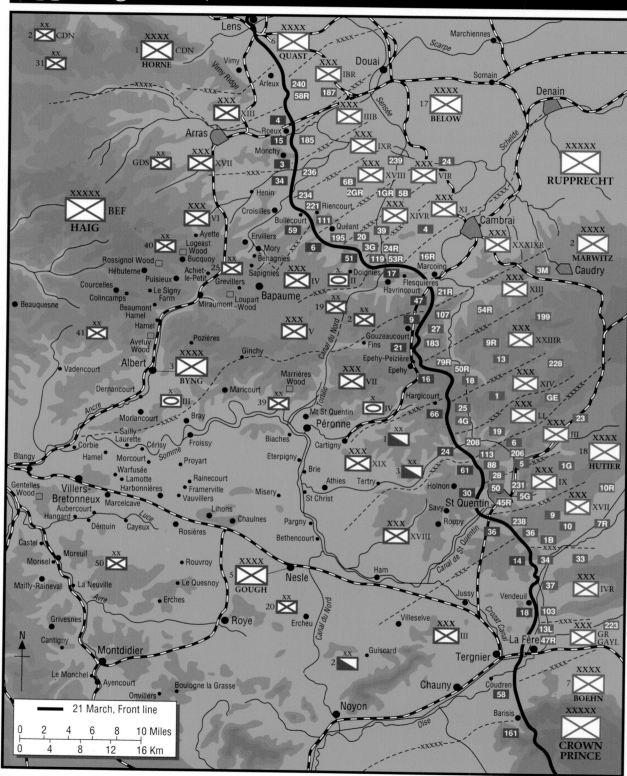

For close to 40,000 casualties (10,851 killed) Ludendorff had captured 98½ square miles of France including 46 ruined villages. His armies had caused the BEF about 38,500 losses (including around 21,000 prisoners of war, many being wounded), destroyed or captured between 502 and 522 guns, at least 4 tanks, and forced it to retreat from another 40 square miles and eleven villages. The combined casualty toll (though not the killed) surpassed the first day of the 1916 Somme battles (and probably any other day's fighting in history for which there are reliable figures). And by a remarkable coincidence Ludendorff had made the exact territorial gains in area and villages that Haig and Fayolle had needed 140 days to wrest from the German Army in 1916.

Yet, as Middlebrook also comments, Ludendorff had only broken clean through the Battle Zone on a quarter of the frontage attacked, and his pincers had not met behind the Flesquières salient. Below realistically reported the main battle still to come, and his superior, Crown Prince Rupprecht, thought Fifth Army had been caught in mid-retreat. For all generals the day began a mind-wrenching time of readjustment from the static certainties of 1915-17. Hutier's newest division, the 238th, had made the record advance of 4½ miles.

The fog made air operations a slow starter on the 21st. Widespread flying and fighting took place in the afternoon when Fokkers were able to make the ground attacks intended from the start. At least six German regimental histories attest to the

◄ *Opposing Forces, 21 March 1918 – the line up of divisions and higher formations on the opening day. Altogether 38 front-line German divisions faced 21 British, but only 32 of the former went over the top at 9.40 a.m. against sixteen British. Below's two northernmost corps and Marwitz's one opposite Flesquières did not join in the infantry attack. Nevertheless by the day's end Gough's Fifth Army had identified 40 German divisions in action against it; in other words, Marwitz and Hutier committed all but six of their divisions, even* half *of their third line. Only five British reserve divisions came into action on the 21st.*

▼*British officer prisoners of war are marched through Cambrai in March 1918. Most of these officers are subalterns or lieutenants. The diamond shoulder insignia of the first row could indicate the second brigade of a division. The BEF's officer losses in the week to 27 March were a 1914-18 record – 6,325. Total officer casualties for the battle rose to 8,344, of which 2,795 were listed as 'missing'. (IWM Q51462)*

efficacy of British bombing or air-directed shelling. By the end of the day, 36 squadrons of the Royal Flying Corps had been engaged, including its II Brigade from Flanders, and it had lost 16 aircraft (German claim 19) and aircrew, claiming 14 German (their figure 8). The Red Baron's unit, however, was one of those unable to take off. Air reconnaissance, including that from balloons, helped both sides, but the conditions largely thwarted British plans for artillery observation aircraft. The German *Infanterieflieger* and balloons tracked the advance by finding the troops' white cloths on captured positions. That night German bombers struck seven major French railway stations.

22 March: Gough retreats, Byng holds

The BEF Chief of Staff, for one, and despite Gough's protestations to the contrary, thought Ludendorff would not follow up on the second day. The German advance resumed at 4 a.m., despite the continued thick fog, the thousand-odd casualties each first line division had sustained on the 21st, and the inevitable delay in other than organic divisional artillery support. In the old Fifth

▲*Part of a batch of 4,000 British Third Army prisoners captured in the Bapaume-Arras sector (the German Seventeen and Second Armies claimed 2,300 and 4,000 prisoners respectively on 21 March) await the train to Germany at a railhead, perhaps Douai. Headgear includes steel helmet liners, woollen cap comforters, and the ubiquitous 'tin hat'.*

▶ *Top: Death in the Rear Zone. This British group have made their last stand in a pathetic scrape of a trench with a Vickers machine-gun and at least one Lee-Enfield rifle. The*

German cameraman's shadow shows in the spring sunshine, and on the skyline of the typical chalky, rolling terrain can be seen German horse-drawn transport. (IWM Q23683)

▶*German cavalry (Ulanen) cross British Battle Zone trenches west of St. Quentin. A dead British lance-corporal lies to the left of a bipod-mounted Lewis Gun. Except on 26 March, pursuing German horsemen were more prominent in Allied rumours than in actual fact.*

Army Forward Zone, five British redoubts fought on, the last only falling at 5 p.m. Before breakfast Gough received the welcome news that a III Corps appeal to its southern neighbour, the French Sixth Army, had obtained Pétain's release of 125th Division to Butler's area via Chauny.

Weather: fog

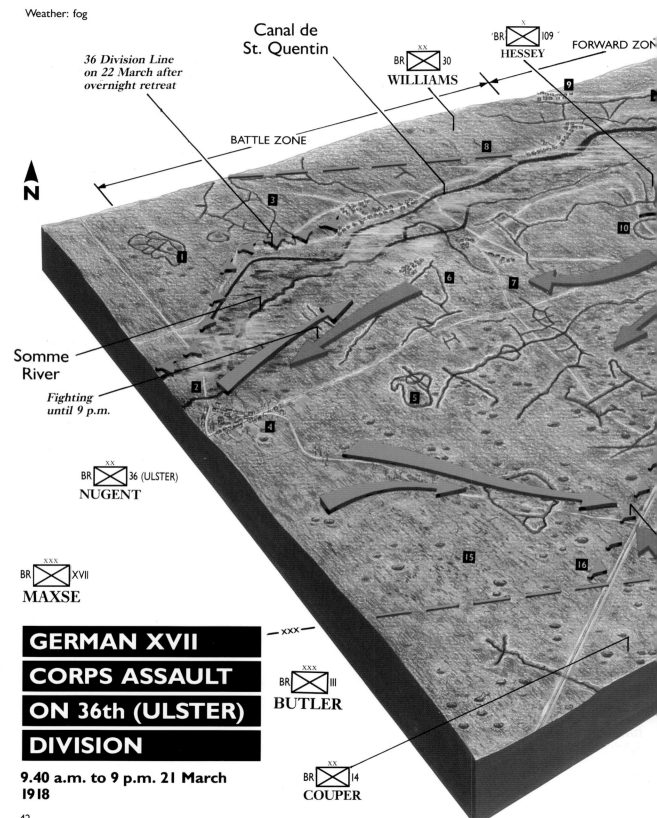

Canal de
St. Quentin

*36 Division Line
on 22 March after
overnight retreat*

BATTLE ZONE

FORWARD ZONE

BR ☒ 109 HESSEY

BR ☒ 30 WILLIAMS

N

Somme
River

*Fighting
until 9 p.m.*

BR ☒ 36 (ULSTER) NUGENT

BR ☒ XVII MAXSE

**GERMAN XVII
CORPS ASSAULT
ON 36th (ULSTER)
DIVISION**

**9.40 a.m. to 9 p.m. 21 March
1918**

BR ☒ III BUTLER

BR ☒ 14 COUPER

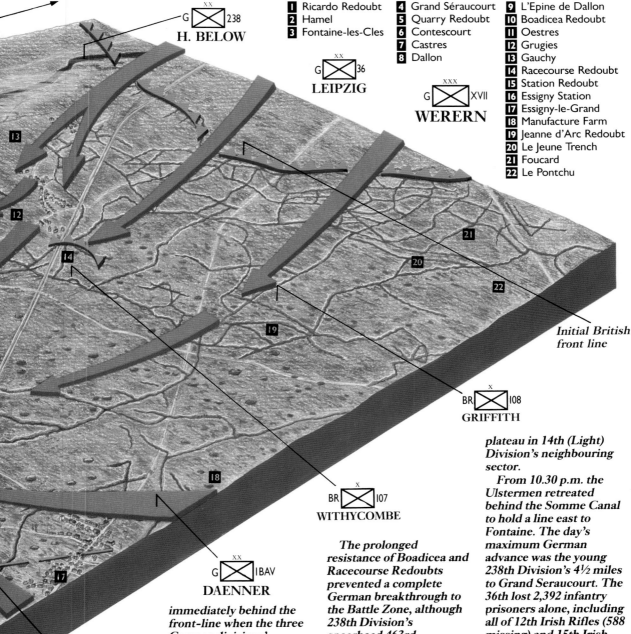

G ⊠ 238
H. BELOW

1 Ricardo Redoubt
2 Hamel
3 Fontaine-les-Cles

4 Grand Séraucourt
5 Quarry Redoubt
6 Contescourt
7 Castres
8 Dallon

9 L'Epine de Dallon
10 Boadicea Redoubt
11 Oestres
12 Grugies
13 Gauchy
14 Racecourse Redoubt
15 Station Redoubt
16 Essigny Station
17 Essigny-le-Grand
18 Manufacture Farm
19 Jeanne d'Arc Redoubt
20 Le Jeune Trench
21 Foucard
22 Le Pontchu

G ⊠ 36
LEIPZIG

G ⊠ XVII
WERERN

Initial British front line

BR ⊠ 108
GRIFFITH

BR ⊠ 107
WITHYCOMBE

Evening line

G ⊠ IBAV
DAENNER

German XVII Corps assault on 36th (Ulster) Division. The first day's fighting in a typical British Fifth Army divisional sector, south of St. Quentin. Nine anti-tank 18pdrs were overrun

immediately behind the front-line when the three German divisions' infantry regiments assaulted 36th Division's three front-line battalions. Only three of their front-line posts resisted until 1 p.m. or later. The first Stosstruppen reached the Forward Zone's line of redoubts by 10 a.m., and the fog thwarted the defenders' artillery barrage until 12.05 p.m.

The prolonged resistance of Boadicea and Racecourse Redoubts prevented a complete German breakthrough to the Battle Zone, although 238th Division's spearhead 463rd Regiment captured Contescourt around 12.30 p.m. The three British reserve battalions near Grand Seraucourt reinforced the incomplete Battle Zone's defenders and, especially to the south, formed a line along the railway against 1st Bavarian Division's capture of the Essigny

plateau in 14th (Light) Division's neighbouring sector.

From 10.30 p.m. the Ulstermen retreated behind the Somme Canal to hold a line east to Fontaine. The day's maximum German advance was the young 238th Division's 4½ miles to Grand Seraucourt. The 36th lost 2,392 infantry prisoners alone, including all of 12th Irish Rifles (588 missing) and 15th Irish Rifles plus 252 prisoners from Boadicea Redoubt (2nd Royal Inniskilling Fusiliers). All three of these overrun battalions lost their COs captured. The division's killed numbered 267. Total losses must have been over half the 6,109 casualties sustained during Kaiserschlacht.

◄The British 4th Guards Brigade (31st Division), composed of 3rd and 4th Battalions, Grenadier Guards, and 3rd Battalion, the Coldstream Guards, under Brigadier-General Lord Ardee (wounded 27 March), embarking in lorries before 9 a.m. on 22 March north-west of Arras. They had an approximately 20-mile journey to Boiry St. Martin (due south of Arras) to reinforce VI Corps just west of the Green Line. A battalion's stretcher-bearer section is marching by the vehicles. The Guards' tall and confident manner was soon reflected in their major contribution to Third Army's resistance. On 25 March the brigade complained that British artillery fire was not allowing proper use of the rifle.

◄A British Third Army Casualty Clearing Station (CCS) near Bapaume on 22 March with many head-wound cases. A CCS (Fifth Army had ten) was usually 20 miles behind the front, receiving patients from the corps-level Main Dressing Station and sending them, after surgery, by ambulance train to Base General Hospital. The BEF's Royal Army Medical Corps had 45,180 personnel on 1 March.

At 10.45 a.m. Gough formally instructed his corps commanders to make fighting retreats to the Rear Zone if pressure warranted it but stipulated that they must keep in touch with each other and the flanking armies. Around noon, Maxse of XVIII Corps prematurely ordered his command to march nine miles back to the Somme because he saw the Green Line as a signboarded token line already threatened by the morning's German pressure on his 36th Division. This formation lay in an awkward salient on the St. Quentin Canal salient owing to Butler's pull-back during the night behind the Crozat Canal.

Watts' XIX Corps, strengthened by 1st Cavalry Division, faced the renewed attacks of Marwitz's left wing, starting with a three-hour bombardment. The British 66th Division was driven fighting from its Battle Zone; seven of its detachments broke out of encirclement. Six tanks and dismounted hussars counter-attacked at noon, temporarily easing the pressure, but at 12.45 p.m. Watts ordered his two original divisions to retreat behind 50th Division, now frantically digging in along eight miles of the Rear Zone Green Line.

Six of Marwitz's divisions renewed the assault on Lieutenant-General Sir Walter Congreve's VII Corps. The already hard-hit 16th Irish Division repelled five massed assaults in five hours; it seems that von Kathen's XXIII Reserve Corps in its haste to capture untaken first day objectives was already discarding infiltration tactics. Its 79th Reserve Division joined the 183rd in efforts to storm the 'flood breaker' village of Epehy-Peizière from a Leicester brigade of 21st Division. Only after 1 p.m. did the strongpoint fall, and only fifteen of the 200-strong British rearguard were found unwounded.

Hutier threw in six divisions against Butler's precarious Crozat Canal line. Mortar and machine-gun fire covered the German attempts to cross the 20–30-yard obstacle; they made the first breach at noon in Tergnier, securing a sizeable bridgehead by around 7.30 p.m. Six miles to the north at Jussy, 1st Bavarian Division failed three times to storm across. The regular 2nd Cavalry Division proved a stiffener: not only did its eighteen 13-pounders check the further advance of General der Infanterie Freiherr von Gayl's

Gruppe, but its commander replaced the first British general to collapse under the strain, the GOC 14th Division.

Below's progress against Byng fell far short of Ludendorff's wishes. The 17th Division smashed all XI Corps attacks at the shoulder of the Flesquières salient. To the north, IV Corps held fast to a six-mile gap beginning just south of the Albert–Cambrai highway. One field artillery brigade (24 guns) fired 20,600 shells over open sights, destroying a German battery, and laid smoke for an evening counter-attack by 25 Mark IV tanks. This largest armoured blow of the battle, falling on the German 24th Reserve Division, effectively plugged the gap in Third Army's centre and, although sixteen tanks failed to return, Below's gain during the day had only been a mile and a half, 5,541 prisoners and 48 guns.

Haldane's VI Corps had been able to relieve the battered 59th Division by the 40th, and this formation fought in the Battle Zone most of the day until forced on to the Green Line by IV Corps' fall-back and 2nd Guard Reserve Division's night storming of Mory village. Even so, less than 300 survivors of 177th Brigade (59th Division) disputed possession until the early hours. The 34th Division still clung to the rear of its Battle Zone having lost Henin Hill to 6th Bavarian Division which then suffered grievously from its own artillery shelling the mêlée. The strongly posted 3rd Division remained in its Arras bastion Forward Zone, although 15th Scottish Division voluntarily evacuated a now-overlooked Monchy Hill to the north.

At 6.30 p.m. Gough visited Byng at Albert to ensure their armies kept touch, the latter ordering V Corps farther back in its salient and a brigade to link his 47th Division with Gough's 9th. Haig, for the first time, really intervened in the battle, seeing that the BEF was in danger of being split. At 11.30 p.m. GHQ ordered Byng to keep touch with Gough even if it meant retreating to the Tortille river line level with Péronne and west of the Green Line. Right on the British armies' boundary, an enterprising German 27th Division regimental commander had occupied Fins at nightfall, thus threatening the Flesquières salient from the south.

Situation 23 March 1918

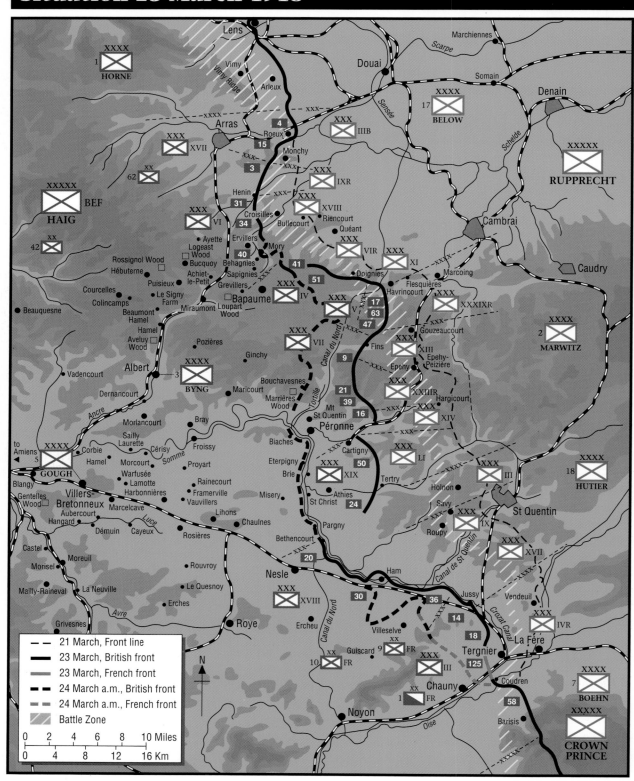

Lens
Marchiennes
Vimy
Douai
Scarpe
Somain
XXXX 1 HORNE
Arleux
Vimy Ridge
XXXX 17 BELOW
Denain
Arras
Roeux
4
XXX XVII
15
Monchy
3
62 xx
Sensée
XXX IIIB
Schelde
XXXXX RUPPRECHT
Cambrai
XXX IXR
Henin
31
XXX VI
34
Croisilles
Bullecourt
Riencourt
Quéant
XXX XVIII
XXXXX BEF HAIG
Ayette
Logeast Wood
Ervillers
Mory
40
XXX VIR
XXX XI
Doignies
42 xx
Rossignol Wood
Hébuterne
Bucquoy
Behagnies
Achiet-le-Petit
41
Sapignies
Grevillers
51
Marcoing
Caudry
Courcelles
Colincamps
Le Signy Farm
Puisieux
Bapaume
XXX IV
Flesquières
Havrincourt
XXX XXXIXR
Beauquesne
Miraumont
Loupart Wood
XXX V
17
63
Gouzeaucourt
MARWITZ 2
Beaumont Hamel
Hamel
Aveluy Wood
Pozières
XXX VII
47
Fins
XXX XIII
Epehy-Peizière
Albert
Ginchy
9
Epehy
Vadencourt
3 BYNG
Maricourt
Bouchavesnes
Marrières Wood
21
39
XXX XXIIIR
Hargicourt
Dernancourt
Ancre
Morlancourt
Bray
Mt St Quentin
16
Péronne
XXX XIV
to Amiens
5 GOUGH
Corbie
Hamel
Sailly Laurette
Cérisy
Froissy
Proyart
Biaches
Eterpigny
Brie
Cartigny
XXX LI
50
Tertry
XXX III
18 HUTIER
Blangy
Gentelles Wood
Villers-Bretonneux
Warfusée
Lamotte
Harbonnières
Marcelcave
Rainecourt
Framerville
Vauvillers
Misery
XXX XIX
Athies
St Christ
24
Holnon
Savy
St Quentin
Aubercourt
Hangard
Démuin
Cayeux
Luce
Rosières
Lihons
Chaulnes
Pargny
Roupy
XXX IX
Castel
Moreuil
Morisel
Mailly-Raineval
La Neuville
Avre
Erches
Bethencourt
20
Nesle
Ham
Jussy
Vendeuil
XXX XVII
Grivesnes
Roye
Ercheu
Canal du Nord
XXX XVIII
30
Villeselve
14
Guiscard
9 xx
XXX FR
La Fère
XXX IVR
7 BOEHN
10 xx
XXX FR
36
18
Tergnier
125
Chauny
1 xx FR
XXX III
Coudren
58
Noyon
Oise
Barisis
XXXXX CROWN PRINCE

Legend:
- 21 March, Front line
- 23 March, British front
- 23 March, French front
- 24 March a.m., British front
- 24 March a.m., French front
- Battle Zone

N

0 2 4 6 8 10 Miles
0 4 8 12 16 Km

French troops had begun to impinge on the battle area, 125th Division sending one regiment briefly into action, while 1st Cavalry and 9th Infantry Divisions came up from debussing points near Noyon. Général Pellé's V Corps was intending to relieve Butler's III Corps during the coming night.

Air power's most significant contribution to the day was from a German night bomber that hit XIX Corps HQ around 9 p. m.; Congreve did not learn of his neighbour's withdrawal for another seven hours. Although seventeen RFC squadrons had to shift bases, four had flown on ground attack, often at 65 feet, and the German air force lost three aircraft in so doing. British losses were 30 aircraft (all causes; German claim 19) to 31 claimed kills (German admitted loss 11) along the whole front. British night bombing (811 light bombs) destroyed at least two ammunition dumps.

23 March: Ludendorff Widens his Aims

The third morning of Ludendorff's offensive saw its conceiver make a radical change of strategy after studying the previous day's accounts and receiving the first news of the day, including air reports of massive BEF traffic retreating westwards. At 9.30 a.m. he set his armies' objectives once the line Bapaume–Péronne–Ham was shortly achieved: Below was to attack vigorously towards Arras–St. Pol, i.e., to swing round Arras from the west; Marwitz was to advance on Miraumont-Lihons, i.e., *on both sides of the Somme*; and Hutier was to march for Chaulnes–Noyon, sending strong forces across the Somme via Ham. In other words, Ludendorff prescribed divergent axes of advance to his forces, which were not in the original plan, because he believed the breakout and exploitation phase was beginning against the beaten British.

He expanded his intentions to the Crown

Princes' chiefs of staff that afternoon as being 'to separate the French and British by a rapid advance on both sides of the Somme' and talked blithely about driving the British into the sea with Seventeenth and Sixth Armies and turning the whole BEF front. Furthermore Hutier was to gain the line Amiens–Montdidier–Noyon and advance south-west against the French. These were three very different strategic objectives.

In particular, Marwitz's weaker central army was no longer to be reinforced from Hutier's right wing but still had to push down astride the Somme for Amiens and keep touch with Hutier and Below. The victorious Hutier, already given three more divisions, was to get two more from Seventh Army on his southern flank. Others have argued that the unprecedented scale of success on a 50-mile front warranted such grandiose opportunistic aims, but even Hutier's progress depended on men, vehicles and horses pressing forward relentlessly along crowded roads. The Kaiser had no doubts: he returned to Berlin shouting that the English were utterly defeated.

The persistent mist rose at 11.30 a.m. Already Hutier had got seven divisions across the Crozat Canal. The first French counter-attack, at dawn, by about 3,000 infantry with only 35 rounds per man, reached Tergnier's outskirts only to break when ammunition ran out. British and French were forced back in fierce fighting through a large series of woods up to 2½ miles south-west of the canal line. By mid-afternoon dismounted cuirassiers of 1st Dismounted Cavalry Division were sustaining the Allied line, and before nightfall British III Corps' assorted scratch forces were in reserve except for 14th 'Division'.

Maxse's four divisions and 264 guns had marched throughout the night, but the Somme river/canal line proved no safe refuge. The Ham bridgehead and its brigade of 30th Division succumbed by 10 a.m. to an infiltrating attack by the German second-line 231st Division. To the east, 5th Guard Reserve Division crossed an unblown rail bridge under fire. Maxse's riposte could only muster 200 men from six 61st Division units who were soon halted by German machine-gun fire. As night fell, XVIII Corps' right flank was up to three miles from its supposedly fixed line.

◄The situation on 23 March 1918. The third morning found Gough's Fifth Army clinging precariously to the Somme-Crozat Canal line, with the first French troops coming up from the *south. A dangerous gap was appearing between Gough's VII Corps and Byng's V Corps, and the latter's Army had finally been driven from most of its Battle Zone.*

◄ *British Fifth Army heavy artillery ammunition limbers and wagon transport take to a ploughed field to pass a burning lorry near Nesle west of the Somme, 23 March. The lorry bas a 6in 26cwt howitzer hitched to it. A battery of whatever type of artillery had twelve general-service (GS) wagons; this one is carrying fodder. The vehicles are probably supporting part of XVIII Corps' 51 heavy guns in action that day, two heavy brigades (regiments) were north-east of Nesle supporting 20th Division. (IWM Q10803)*

◄ *German Eighteenth Army Foot Artillery 210mm howitzers in action near Nesle. Hutier's army began the battle with eight of these powerful pieces, which fired an improved Model 1916 1841b shell over 5.8 miles at up to two rounds a minute. (IWM Q55242)*

◄ *Troops of the British 20th (Light) Division build barricades in Nesle, 23 March. The town, Fifth Army's HQ until that day, was also Maxse's XVIII Corps HQ until a morning move to Roye. Nesle actually fell around 4 p.m. on the 25th when the newly-arrived and shell-deficient French 22nd Division gave way to the much stronger German XXV Reserve Corps using its 206th and 50th Divisions. (IWM Q10800)*

▶ *A Royal Garrison Artillery caterpillar tractor pulls a camouflaged British 6in heavy gun to the rear near Bapaume on 23 March. This strange vehicle has certainly startled the horse on the left. The BEF had 100 6in guns for four-gun batteries on 2 March 1918 and lost at least nine captured to Ludendorff's offensives. Another 69 were delivered to France in March and April. (IWM Q8608)*

▶ *Fifth Army's evacuation of Péronne, 23 March. An Expeditionary Force Canteen store building has been set on fire, and laden soldiers of VII Corps are denying items, notably a box of Bovril and Huntley biscuits, to the advancing foe. That same day a hospital train evacuated wounded from Péronne as it burnt and military police prevented traffic jams. During the afternoon, 16th (Irish) Division retreated through the southern part of the riverside town, which the German 4th Guard Division reoccupied after its year in BEF hands. (IWM Q10806)*

▶ *British Third Army wounded discard their weapons and equipment while queuing at an Advanced Dressing Station (ADS) near Bapaume on 23 March. Normally, at least two miles from the front, patients came by ambulance, stretcher-bearer or as walking wounded from the Regimental Aid Post. The next stage was transfer to the Corps Main Dressing Station. (IWM Q8650)*

►*A French 251st Regiment infantryman in 'Lanciers' body armour.*

▼*A 1917 British Mills bomber with Chemico body shield. Such trench warfare specialists were used in the long winter months before Kaiserschlacht, especially to mount frequent night raids aimed at identifying German units in the opposing line.*

▼*A German Stosstrupp (stormtrooper) with body armour. Before Kaiserschlacht, from 8 December 1917, the Germans made an estimated 225 trench raids gaining 62 unit identifications, especially against the Ypres salient and Third Army front.*

▶ *Third Army Royal Garrison Artillerymen unload 12in howitzer shells from a 60cm light railway near Bapaume, 23 March, probably in IV Corps area. A lorry column is waiting to take the ammunition to the guns. Third Army had fifteen rail-mounted 12in howitzers (Fifth Army had ten). The BEF's 12in howitzers fired 9,030 rounds during the battle period. Ludendorff's unprecedentedly deep spring advances captured six of these rear-support guns. (IWM Q8610)*

XIX Corps' defence was bolstered by the arrival of the veteran 8th (Regular) Division, from Second Army in Flanders, to hold eight miles of the Somme. Before that 50th and 24th Divisions successfully disengaged from east of the river, although 1st Cavalry Division lost horses, and five tanks were abandoned being unable to cross the obstacle. Around 9 p.m. 70 men of 8th Division expelled 120 Germans from a bridgehead at Pargny, taking four machine-guns; a similar bid at St. Christ was also repulsed.

Congreve's VII Corps and 263 guns began 23 March on its Green Line but was soon absorbed in the complex task of defending, evacuating and crossing the Péronne area. Frequently the artillery covered the retreat after the weary infantry had hastily fallen back, as at Mont St. Quentin around 4 p.m. when 39th Division relinquished this key high ground covering the town. The day's losses included 31 guns and at the close VII Corps lay in four segments split by the Somme. Worse, a gap of at least 3,000 yards had opened between Congreve's 9th Division and Third Army.

Byng's third order to V Corps in the Flesquières salient had finally emptied this sector in an orgy of burning dumps, but divergently away from Gough, and in the confusion 47th Division had been unable to perform a linking role. Harper's IV Corps fell back far less, covered by its destructive artillery in two powerful groups and ending the day still on the Green Line, although five battalions

were lost under Below's attacks. Haldane's VI Corps actually made three counter-attacks that retook Mory for about seven hours and remained on the Green Line thanks partly due to Generalleutnant Albrecht's difficulties in getting heavy guns forward.

That afternoon Haig had bestirred himself to visit Gough at Villers-Brettoneux, Fifth Army Headquarters. Told of 45 German divisions on the Army's now 47-mile front, he somewhat obviously commented to its commander that more men were needed. At 4 p.m. Pétain visited Haig at Dury (Advanced GHQ, south of Amiens) to be met by a request for twenty French divisions to concentrate around Amiens. The Frenchman was perhaps too stunned to answer, having already reported that Fayolle was bringing up thirteen divisions to Gough's right, not merely the six earmarked. It was agreed that Fayolle would take over Fifth Army's command up to the Somme in 30 hours' time.

Pétain, expecting a German attack in Champagne on the 26th or earlier, was so rattled that he told Clemenceau at dinner that Ludendorff would beat the Allies in detail. Meanwhile Haig's imperturbability was sufficiently shaken after this meeting for GHQ to issue an order at 5 p.m. requiring the Somme line to be held 'at all costs' when its integrity was in fact already broken. More realistically at 7.30 p.m. the Field Marshal met his unengaged army commanders. General Sir

Herbert Plumer unselfishly agreed to spare three more divisions, all high-quality Australian ones. Furthermore Byng had ordered a rear 'Purple Line' to be fortified along the old 1916 Ancre sector.

Air fighting had reached a new peak. The RFC lost 32 aircraft (German claim 24) in the battle area and claimed 36 German (admitted loss 11), a figure at least reflected by German accounts of their army cooperation and battle flights' diffi-

culties, as well as the loss of Ludendorff's stepson. British ground troops accounted for at least two German aircraft, and XIX Corps in particular did benefit from air-directed artillery fire plus bombing.

24 March: Back to the Old Somme Battlefield

On Palm Sunday the Somme region still lay under thick fog until 11 a.m. This did not delay Hutier's

▲*German Eighteenth Army artillery advances down a sunken road before Ham (on the Somme), about 23 March. The gun limbers are passing a wheeled transport column, perhaps a Corps Train Battalion. The thinness and small size of the horses is apparent. (IWM Q29951)*

◄*British XVIII Corps infantry line a Somme track in the Nesle sector, 24 March. Nesle's 12th century abbey church is just visible in the morning mist on the skyline to the right. The troops may be from the 184th Brigade (61st Division), in reserve that morning south-west of the town in the 20th Division sector. (IWM Q10786)*

▶ *A cheerful US sergeant of the 6th Engineers at Roye on 24 March sitting on a load of trestle supports. The next day his unit was incorporated to fight as infantry in Carey's Force on the Amiens Defence Line. (IWM Q10791)*

barrages or infantry attacks with thirteen divisions. From 6 a.m. three of them struck the much-jumbled Franco-British line in III Corps area, now under Général Pellé. The French 1st Dismounted Cavalry Division was driven, often ammunition-less, from half-a-dozen villages by noon, and its retreat forced back 9th and 125th Divisions on either flank. The British 58th Division survivors north of the Oise must have been very relieved to retreat with the latter formation south of that river by evening. All told, Général de Division Maurice Gamelin's 9th Division retreated five miles albeit to a more compact line which 55th Division had entered.

British authors tend to diminish the French intervention and point up the irony of Fifth Army units covering the troops that were supposed to relieve them, but it must be remembered their allies were entering a losing battle after many hours in crowded trucks, with time for sizing up the situation. In fact Pellé was able to pull 14th Division and three cavalry brigades into reserve, 158 British artillery pieces remaining to support the as yet undergunned *poilus*. Such was the confusion in this area that Crown Prince Rupprecht was informed last thing on the 23rd that the US 26th Division had been identified as well as the French!

Maxse exercised firmer control of his corps battle than the now largely redundant Butler, having told General Robillot that XVIII Corps should not be relieved piecemeal by the slowly arriving French 22nd and 62nd Divisions. Seven of Hutier's divisions attacked, the two from the Ham bridgehead destroying two battalions of 36th (Ulster) Division only to be momentarily checked by a cavalry charge at Villeselve. There after 2 p.m. 150 troopers of 6th Cavalry Brigade galloped across 600 yards, despite machine-gun fire from the left, and sabred 88 Guardsmen of the 5th Guard Division, taking 107 prisoners and three machine-guns for 73 casualties. The heartened Irish infantry held the village for another two hours. On the left the previously unattacked 20th Division lining the Somme faced a 30-minute air-directed barrage and fourteen fresh German battalions (six being *Stosstruppen*). After many small actions, the defenders retreated about two miles to the Canal du Nord line covering Nesle.

A new German corps, General der Infanterie von Winckler's XXV Reserve, skilfully directed 28th and 1st Guard Divisions' crossing at Bethen-court via footbridges from 4 a.m. By 5 p. m. this bridgehead included Pargny despite Major-General William Heneker's 8th Division's best efforts with air support and thus drove a wedge between Watts and Maxse that opened a mile gap. XIX Corps was being levered off the Somme even though only one other German crossing in its 8-mile front even got a foothold, south of Péronne. Learning of this penetration at 4.30 p.m., Gough planned a bold Allied converging counterstroke for the morrow using four of Maxse's brigades and the new French 22nd Division to regain the Somme line at Pargny. Fayolle, and Robillot approved this plan.

The British plight was today far worse north of the Somme, even though Congreve regained touch with Third Army. His corps retreated up to six miles despite a verbally ordered, magnificent last stand by the 500-strong South African Brigade. Surrounded north of Marrières Wood, it fought for nearly eight hours to the last round against the German 199th and 9th Reserve Divisions. Brigadier-General F.S. Dawson and fewer than a hundred South Africans were captured around 5 p. m. but learnt Marwitz's advance had been delayed for over seven hours by a traffic jam east of Bouchavesnes. The other two brigades of 9th Division mustered barely a battalion in number, while 21st 'Division' fell back on Hunt's Force (8 battalions) one of several ad hoc forces the BEF had had to organize since the 23rd. Only the arrival of 35th Division from Flanders and the transfer of 1,000 1st Cavalry Division mounted troops across the river gave Congreve troops to man a line now well inside the old 1916 Somme battlefield.

Byng's two southern corps had also swung back, in a great chaotic north-west wheel by brigades south of Bapaume and its burning supply dump. By 2.30 p.m. General der Infanterie von Stäbs' XXXIX Reserve Corps had thrust vigorously into a now four-mile gap between the British armies, sometimes marching in parallel. Fanshawe lost contact with two of his divisions, and even brigadier-generals on horseback (two of whom were killed or captured in the process) were hard-pressed to find their units in the 1916 crater fields. Not until well after dawn on the 25th did the two British armies regain tenuous touch.

At 7 p.m. Harper ordered his IV Corps to retreat after Generalleutnant von dem Borne's VI Reserve Corps had finally broken the Green Line. The 41st Division's rearguards were covered by a six-tank counter-attack; the 19th and 51st Divisions covered each other's retreat past a heavily-shelled Bapaume, but 60 guns blocked Achiet-le-Petit overnight to the west. Fortunately for these weary troops, the embussed 16,287-strong 42nd Division was being committed in support. VI Corps, with the Guards Division still in its Battle Zone, only had to swing back its right to conform with Harper in spite of furious and costly attacks by six of Below's divisions.

At 8 p.m. Haig visited Byng to stress the vital Arras link and tell him that reserves were coming. Three hours later Pétain paid a second visit to his opposite number at Dury. Gough was to come under Fayolle's broad direction now that French troops already held 14½ miles of Fifth Army's 36-mile front. Pétain struck Haig as 'very much upset, almost unbalanced and most anxious' and again mentioned his fears of the main German blow coming in Champagne. Then came the bombshell – he had told Fayolle that afternoon to cover Paris by falling back on Beauvais if the German Crown Prince's advance continued south-west. He then handed over the day's written order to his army groups that stressed maintaining the French Army's integrity and only secondly mentioning liaison with the BEF. To Haig's direct question as to whether he meant to abandon the BEF's right flank, the French general nodded yes and added, 'It is the only thing possible, if the enemy compels the Allies to fall back still farther.'

Haig drove back to Montreuil, his faculties surely electrified by the implications of Allied separation. At 3 a.m. he cabled and then telephoned the War Office asking urgently for General Wilson (CIGS) and Lord Milner to cross the Channel. And, he warned, if 'General Foch or some other determined general who would fight' was not given 'supreme control of operations' the BEF 'must fight its way slowly back covering the Channel ports'. If Pétain had mistakenly got it into his head that Haig meant to retire northwards, he can surely never have dreamt that his colleague would so enthusiastically and urgently propose the elevation of Foch, the Allied northern sector C-in-C of 1914-16. Furthermore Haig then wrote personally to Clemenceau and Foch decrying the Champagne threat and urging that twenty French divisions be concentrated on the Somme.

In the air, the French had made their presence felt. Waves of 20–80 bombers from the Aviation Reserve intervened in Picardy, especially attacking Hutier's horse-drawn transport in sustained operations to the 29th. Anglo-German fighting saw a respective loss of 52 (German claim 23) and 41 (German figure 9) aircraft. The Germans bombed Albert, Amiens and its Longueau rail junction, destroying an ammunition train there that interrupted traffic for at least ten hours.

25 March: Third Army Reels Back

Gough's counterstroke collapsed with the rising mist in the face of Robillot's postponements and a German 8 a.m. assault by the six foremost divisions in the Nesle–Ham bridgehead. They drove the two French divisions back about 2½ miles and from Nesle within eight hours and forced the more tenacious British to conform. By evening Robillot had to retreat another three miles to a line stiffened by cavalry and armoured cars just covering Roye. From this area Maxse forcefully night-marched north-west the 4,000 surviving infantry of his four divisions in order to re-establish the line between the French and XIX Corps. It is sufficient comment on their infantry's 'piteous state' that both French divisional commanders were replaced within four days. Robillot, however, retained Maxse's artillery, as did Pellé Butler's around Noyon.

This III Corps area had also come under Humbert's French Third Army, which had four infantry and a dismounted cavalry division holding

the line with Butler's remnants in support and two new infantry divisions (1st and 35th) arriving near Noyon. Short of ammunition and artillery, this array proved unable to stem Generalleutnant von Conta's prompt and sustained attacks with seven divisions of IV Reserve Corps. The German 33rd Division in particular outflanked Noyon from the

▶ *A lance-corporal of 1/6th Battalion, the Gordon Highlanders (Banff and Donside), 152nd Brigade, 51st Highland Division (Territorial Force, 1st Line) in marching order. The sleeve stripes indicate battalion number and brigade (the senior) by colour. A company of this unit held the right of 152nd Brigade's Forward Zone on 21 March, helping check the German 24th Reserve Division in and outside Boursies despite noon strafing by seventeen aircraft. Another company was in the Battle Zone fight for Doignies. The battalion fought just behind the Green Line on 23-4 March, coming temporarily under a brigade of 19th Division. It retreated past Bapaume on the 24th and fought almost hand-to-hand at Loupart Wood for an hour on 25 March.*

◀ *A British Mark V tank of 2nd Battalion (II Tank Brigade), The Tank Corps, comes through Aveluy on the Ancre (north of Albert) in the Third Army sector on 25 March. The mule-drawn carts seem unperturbed and a lance-corporal's light infantry section takes a breather by the roadside. Other tanks were in action in Third Army area that afternoon, and 2nd Battalion had already made the battle's largest such attack on the 22nd. (IWM Q8639)*

◀ *British Third Army 60-pounder Mark II battery of V Corps in action near La Boiselle (on the Albert-Bapaume road) on the old Somme battlefield, 25 March. One Royal Garrison Artillery gun detachment is trying to sleep through the barrage. This 5in-calibre heavy field gun fired a 60lb shell to 12,300 yards (7 miles) at up to two rounds a minute. Third Army began the battle with 96 such guns in four-gun batteries, and V Corps had 19 of them. On the 25th they helped inflict severe losses on five German divisions' mass assaults. (IWM 8616)*

◀ *French 22nd Division infantry with British 20th Division survivors man a line of newly scraped rifle pits in the Nesle sector, 25 March. The French Lebel rifle weighed over a pound more than the Short Magazine Lee-Enfield, carried eight rounds rather than ten, and was sighted only to a maximum of 2,187 yards instead of 2,800 yards. The Germans attacked at 8 a.m. and the 22nd Division suffered the first of 2,720 casualties. (IWM Q10810)*

west, forcing Pellé's V Corps well south of that town, an eight-mile retreat in the day. Pellé's right wing was forced back over the Oise by 5 p.m.

Ironically, 170 British in reserve (54th Brigade, 18th Division) counter-attacked at 5.30 p.m., retook Baboeuf village in 30 minutes, killed or captured 230 Germans and captured ten machine-guns in order to save a French battery and then acted as rearguard into the small hours. Général Brecard's 1st Dismounted Cavalry Division had sustained 1,343 casualties in three days.

Watts' XIX Corps now stood alone on a thirteen-mile front along the Somme, a mile apart from Third Army (now including VII Corps north of the Somme) and also from Maxse. The German 8 a.m. attack was for a time mistaken as French but still needed three hours to gain two more villages from 8th and 24th Divisions. The German 208th Division required massed machine-guns, 80 guns and four attempts to force the Somme at Eterpigny bridge, making other crossings at Biaches west of Péronne. Not until 4.15 p.m. did Lieutenant-General Watts order a four-mile withdrawal for nightfall to his partially prepared second line. It was achieved by dawn on the 26th, but eight guns were lost under machine-gun fire, and 2nd Middlesex Regiment was 75 per cent destroyed in a tenacious twelve-hour defence of Brie bridge against the German 19th Division. Two other 8th Division battalions cut their way through Misery village with the bayonet.

Overnight XIX Corps, with its six divisions of scarcely 1,000 infantry apiece, had become Gough's only formation in line – on a thirteen-mile front with a three-mile gap from the French and four miles ahead of Third Army.

Byng's command had another dire day and night. The newly included VII Corps was the exception thanks principally to the 'fresh' 35th Division, which stiffened a line on the old Somme battlefield. It held against five separate attacks involving five of Marwitz's divisions, all suffering heavy officer losses. Fanshawe's V Corps, now seventeen miles from its 21 March salient, lay tired, depleted and fragmented with three of its eight brigades mustering only 1,300 men between them. Attacked by five German divisions from first light they were half forced across the Albert–

Bapaume road by 2 p.m. Under German mass attacks that only had infantry gun support, the British fell back fighting to the old 1916 Ancre line by 6 p.m. Eyewitnesses reckoned that von Stäbs' and von Watters' troops suffered the heaviest losses of the March fighting.

Below struck IV Corps with fifteen divisions either side of Bapaume. Most of 19th Division's 2,200 survivors fought six German divisions for over ten hours although forced back on to 51st Division in and around Loupart Wood by 2 p.m. Harper had the new 42nd and 62nd Divisions in support or coming up but at 5.15 p.m. he let his old sadly diminished command, 51st Highland Division, retreat to reorganize behind the new formations. This uncovered the 25th and 41st Division remnants to the north and forced them to conform. Luckily for them, the GOC 42nd Division had enterprisingly counter-attacked at around 1 p.m. with seven tanks (five being lost in the process) and perhaps 300 infantry from Logeast Wood. This action delayed von dem Borne's VI Reserve Corps for over an hour. To the north the 42nd's 1/10th Manchester Regiment anchored the corps line in Ervillers. Aided by two Vickers guns firing 5,000 rounds apiece, this battalion repulsed eight mass assaults by 2nd Guard Reserve Division. Haldane's VI Corps was hardly troubled except by artillery and air attacks.

During a stormy and hail-ridden night, 19th Division's staff officers along the Purple Line collected more than 4,000 stragglers including 600 men of their own. One company found itself with 900 troops. Nevertheless, before dusk a German 24th Division patrol got across the Ancre near Beaumont Hamel. About 6 p.m. Byng had telephoned his corps commanders ordering a night retreat behind the Bray–Albert–Ancre–Puisieux–Bucquoy line. Written orders took hours longer to reach headquarters and even longer to reach divisional and brigade commanders, but they were fulfilled by 10 a.m. next day in a magnificent effort by staffs. At 9 p.m. Byng switched the arriving New Zealand Division to support IV Corps west of the Ancre. Even so, a 4½-mile gap remained between IV and V Corps.

Ludendorff seems to have sensed Byng's plight, for that morning he had verbally ordered

Situation 26 March 1918

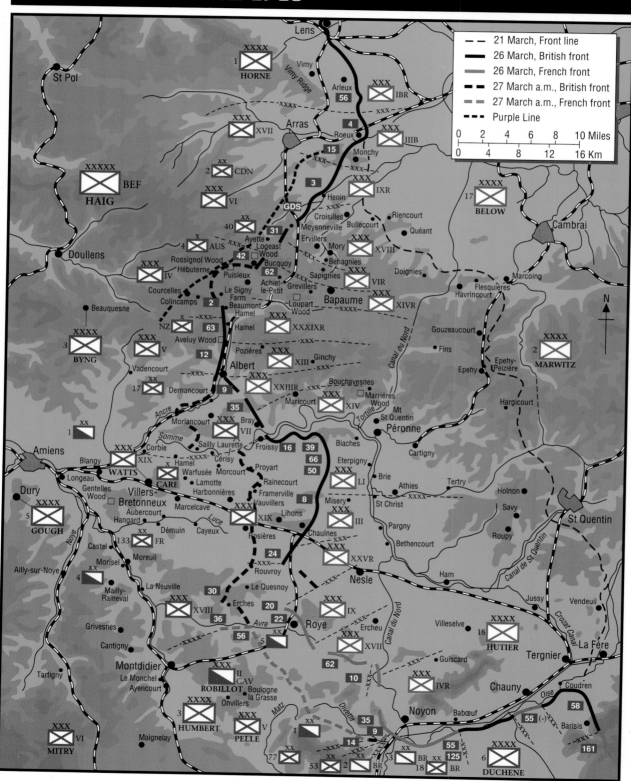

Legend:
- 21 March, Front line
- 26 March, British front
- 26 March, French front
- 27 March a.m., British front
- 27 March a.m., French front
- Purple Line

Scale:
0 2 4 6 8 10 Miles
0 4 8 12 16 Km

Kühl to make sure Marwitz shifted forces north-west on Miraumont to aid crossing the Ancre. Furthermore the 'Mars' attack astride the Scarpe was fixed for the 28th.

The 'flap' in the Allied High Commands continued. The CIGS, General Wilson, reached GHQ at 11 a.m. to be told that French help was essential. He went on to Pétain at Compiègne. Haig drove to Abbeville expecting to find Foch, Clemenceau, and Lord Milner at 4 p.m. Only Foch's chief of staff, General Maxime Weygand, turned up and was given a note by Haig for the French prime minister urging that Pétain's reserves be concentrated north of the Somme near Amiens. At Compiègne, Milner and the French leaders, except Pétain, agreed that the Allied armies must stay united. Milner and Clemenceau resolved to meet Haig next morning at Doullens, the BEF C-in-C having arranged to meet his army commanders there at 11 a.m. The newest ally too had been concerned. At 10 p.m. General Pershing visited Pétain at Chantilly, whence GQG had moved that very day ostensibly for fear of air attack. The American, being told of the few French reserves left, offered any of his four divisions rather than form US I Corps as previously planned.

The Royal Flying Corps had thrown itself heart and soul into the ground battle as a result of Major-General Salmond's 11.05 a.m. order 'to bomb and shoot everything they can see' on the German side of the Third Army Grevillers–Maricourt line. Over 100 aircraft of all types, including First Army's I Brigade, responded so that German regimental histories record swarms of 15-30 low-flying airmen attacking them. An élite regiment of 23rd Division lost 133 casualties to three bombs near Athies from No.5 (Naval) Squadron, later that day switched from Gough's sector to Byng's. Night bombers struck Péronne and Bapaume with 287 bombs. German operations suffered from the unprecedented advance causing

airfield and coordination difficulties. The Germans admitted a loss of six aircraft for eight British.

26 March: Foch becomes Allied Generalissimo

Gough, afflicted – on top of everything – by toothache, had prepared for the worst the previous night by ordering the garrisoning and improvement of his eight-mile 'Amiens Defence Line' four miles east of Villers-Bretonneux and fifteen miles east of the city it was to protect. This was in origin a 1915 French trench system. The garrison and refortifiers consisted of 2,900 troops, mainly ten Army engineer companies and 500 US (Railway) Engineers with 92 Lewis and Vickers machine-guns. Major-General George Carey took command late on the 26th, so this last-ditch detachment became Carey's Force, the best known of all the BEF's improvised units.

The French were improvising on a grander scale. On paper General Debeney's First Army was now to come up on Humbert's left and reforge the link with Gough. For the greater part of the day two cavalry divisions fought to cover the 35th and 56th Infantry Divisions coming up by lorry from Montdidier. They also had to sustain the demoralized 22nd and 62nd Divisions' infantry, who steadily yielded ground to six of Hutier's persistent divisions from 4 a.m. Roye fell before noon despite strenuous shooting from the French cavalry's armoured cars. Up to 2,400 mounted men of British 2nd Cavalry Division and Harman's Detachment made a dismounted counter-attack south-west of Noyon to aid Gamelin's group and the hard-hit 10th Division. Except directly south of Noyon, where Général de Division Denis Duchêne's Sixth Army lent powerful support from across the Oise, skilful German infiltration had pushed Pellé's and Robillot's Corps back four to five miles. A French tactical study records Kaiserschlacht's only German cavalry attack: two ruinously costly charges on a battalion of 9th Division.

Gough's XVIII and XIX Corps now stood squarely on an 18-mile front in the Santerre Plain extending to the great Somme bend. Maxse's troops retreated north-west covered by a heroic rearguard in Le Quesnoy village. A brigade major

◄ The situation on 26 March 1918, the battle Foch inherited. Plenty of Allied reserves were in motion, but would they arrive in time to seal off

Ludendorff's penetrations before Montdidier, along the Avre, in the Somme-Ancre peninsula and, above all, at Hébuterne?

and 100 all ranks of 7th Duke of Cornwall's Light Infantry with two Lewis guns held on from noon until 6.40 p.m. when eleven survivors got clear. After nightfall six battalions of the German 28th Division did sunder 36th Division's artilleryless line by capturing Erches, but Maxse had successfully redeployed his Corps back between the French and XIX Corps.

Watts had ordered retirement in case of heavy attack the night before, but owing to messengers being lost or killed his orders did not reach brigades until 2½ hours after fighting began, and

withdrawals had already been enforced by six attacking divisions from the flanking corps of Hutier and Marwitz. The five-mile retreat to the selected Rouvroy–Froissy crest line cost 24th Division's 9th East Surreys all 300 men (of whom only 57 were unwounded), but otherwise was achieved albeit in accelerated fashion. British heavy gun shelling of Rainecourt caused a composite battalion to evacuate the village at about 3.30 p.m., enabling Lüttwitz's troops to occupy it and capture neighbouring Framerville. These villages were only a few hundred yards from XIX

◀ *A captured British 6in 26cwt howitzer position with fuzed ammunition and sandbagged dugouts or shelter tarpaulins. Ludendorff captured 147 such weapons in his 1918 offensives. The 6in, designed in 1915, was the BEF's standard and effective medium howitzer. It had a range of 11,600 yards (6.5 miles) with a 100lb shell. Fifth Army began with 262 such howitzers and Third Army had 217. (IWM Q29971)*

◀ *An Allied barricade at Roye on 26 March. The troops displaying sang-froid for the camera are a 28th Cavalry Regiment patrol with lances from the newly-arriving French 5th Cavalry Division, infantry of the French 22nd Division, and British 20th or 61st Division infantrymen. (IWM Q10825)*

Corps' new line, now supported by 445 guns. The 16th Division still held the Somme crossing to the north and demolished all the remaining bridges on Watts' order after 9 p.m. At Watts' request Gough sent fourteen machine-guns (including a Canadian battery) and 350 infantry to reinforce the watch on the river crossings.

Byng's overnight orders to his six corps commanders (the Cavalry Corps now added) stipulated a fall-back line from south-east of Arras via the Purple Line to villages well behind the Ancre, if German pressure forced it. The exhausted Con-

greve understandably interpreted this as permission to retreat from his exposed Albert–Bray sector after a delaying action. The retreat began at about 2.30 p.m. covered by nine tanks. Half-an-hour later Congreve rang his subordinate, Major-General G.M. Franks, countermanding the order because Third Army, owing to the Doullens Conference, had instructed that there was to be no voluntary withdrawal. Franks drove forward on crowded roads to find his troops had already marched over three miles back. Around 4 p.m. at Morlancourt he decided it was too late to reverse

▶ *French refugees with furniture-laden farm carts climb the ridge at Bouzincourt to descend into the untouched country beyond, 26 March. They are passing two British Third Army lorry-mounted, 13-pounder 9cwt anti-aircraft guns, well placed to sweep the skies west of Albert. They could fire to 13,000ft at eight shots a minute or theoretically to over 4½ miles in a horizontal ground role. Most of the gun detachments are resting in a shell crater. A similar battery, opposite St. Quentin on 21 March, was the first ever such British unit to fight in a ground role. That evening (26 March) German aircraft attacked Senlis west of Bouzincourt in the moonlight. Fifth Army's anti-aircraft group claimed seventeen German aircraft in March alone. (IWM Q8637)*

▶ *A British Third Army Mk VII 6in gun in action behind a chalk ridge near Hédauville, 26 March, west of the Ancre. Hédauville (4½ miles north-west of Albert) was in V Corps sector and where New Zealand reserves were arriving that day. This type of gun fired 51,677 shells during the battle period.*

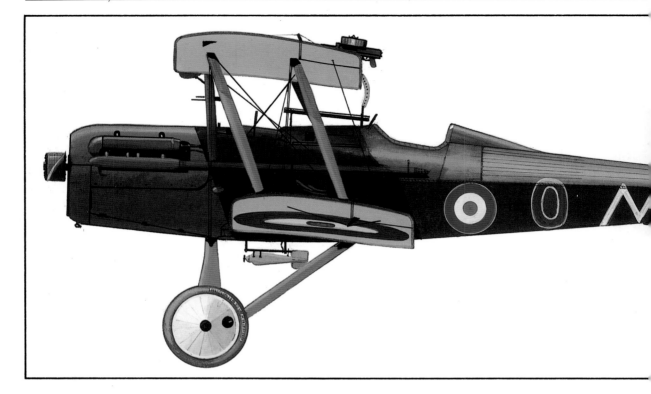

matters. The saga of order, counter-order and disorder continued past midnight. It left only scratch forces of 450 cavalrymen and 2,000 infantry details in the vital Somme–Ancre peninsula five miles *behind* Gough's northern flank. Luckily for them, the equally exhausted German 13th Division remained in Morlancourt while 3rd Australian Division force-marched south.

Fanshawe's V Corps abandoned Albert to hold the high ground west of the Ancre. The German 3rd Marine and 54th Reserve Divisions entered the battered town about 4.30 p.m. but could get no farther against the new 12th Division despite furious night attacks. One British counter-attack netted 50 prisoners and thirteen machine-guns. The situation in IV Corps sector to the north was far more precarious, starting with a gap that 24th (Saxon) Division exploited in the small hours to reach Colincamps, only nineteen miles north-west of Amiens and four miles over the Ancre. Unluckily for them the New Zealand Division came force-marching up from the south by battalions to engage 4th Division from 11 a.m. The latter's noon two-battalion attack on Colincamps seemed to outflank the New Zealanders when twelve

brand-new Whippet tanks suddenly counter-attacked, panicking over 300 infantry and capturing four machine-guns. The Germans bivouacked that night 1½ miles east of Colincamps while the New Zealanders in four successive attacks finally sealed the gap at 6.30 a.m. by linking with 4th Australian Brigade in Hébuterne.

That unit had marched through the midday panic of 'the Point to Point' engendered by the unfamiliar Whippets being falsely reported by British mounted gunner patrols as German tanks or armoured cars. Another mis-identity, of Ford tractor-pulled French ploughs being denied the Boche, helped trigger a transport column exodus that extended to Doullens. The fall of Hébuterne was falsely reported, but in fact 19th Division's 1,800 survivors repulsed all German probes forward. The much-shelled adjoining Rossignol Wood–Bucquoy sector, held by 62nd and 42nd Divisions, threw back six 3rd Guard Division attacks, the last being dispersed by eleven Mark IV tanks.

Haldane's VI Corps had an edgy rumour-rife day in which the Corps Commander on Army orders moved his command post fifteen miles

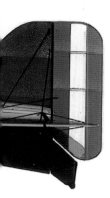

◀ The 28ft wing-span British SE5a single-seat fighter, of late 1917 on, equipped Numbers 41, 56 and 84 Squadrons, RFC, during the battle, i.e., four of the thirteen pure fighter units involved, or about 80 aircraft. Its 200hp Hispano Suiza engine gave a speed of 135mph at 6,500ft, a climb to 10,000ft in 11 minutes and an operational ceiling of 20,000ft with 2½-hour endurance. Armament was a Vickers (400 rounds) above the engine cowling and a Lewis gun (four 97-round drums) above the centre section. Less manoeuvrable than the more famous Sopwith Camel, it was faster and a more stable gun-platform.

close support, including three of Fifth Army's squadrons. The Bapaume area received most of the 1,437 bombs and 228,000 bullets expended. Transport columns and Pozières ammunition dump suffered many hits. Four German battalions 'debussing' on the Roye–Nesle road were hit by bombs. For 50 aircraft lost (German claim only 12), the RFC claimed ten German (their figure 5). Both sides night-bombed, the Germans struck at least two airfields and Amiens, while the British aimed another 1,226 bombs on Albert, Bapaume, Péronne, six Somme battlefield villages, Ham and Cambrai.

west; but his troops only lost Moyenneville after retaking it once from a Bavarian battalion. The 34th and 59th Divisions were pulled right out to rest. Byng's troops had retreated about 22 miles in five days.

In the air, Third Army had the benefit of more than 250 RFC aircraft (27 squadrons) flying in

▼ The 14-ton British Medium Mark A Whippet light tank, designed from December 1916 and first completed in October 1917, made a successful combat début during Kaiserschlacht with 3rd Battalion, the Tank Corps. Its 9ft high fan-ventilated fighting compartment carried three to four Hotchkiss .303in machine-guns behind 5-14mm armour and a crew of four. A twin 45bhp engine could achieve 8.3mph, a veritable sprint for 1916-18 tanks, and fuel carried gave a road range of 80 miles for the 20ft by 8ft 7in vehicle. Trench width crossing ability was 7ft. These characteristics were intended to let the Whippet exploit a breakthrough by heavy tanks. Seven Whippets of 3rd Battalion repeated their 26 March feat by causing 400 casualties to two German infantry battalions that broke through south of Villers-Bretonneux on 24 April in Marwitz's limited A7V-supported offensive towards Amiens.

The Doullens Conference

On the morning of the 26th the Allied 'frocks' and brass-hats gathered at Amiens railway station to drive north to Doullens. Haig had already met three of his four army commanders at 11 a.m. and agreed to hold on for French support south of the Somme. Pétain told his prime minister, 'The Germans will beat the British in open country; after that they'll beat us.' Clemenceau was shocked to the core, telling this to President Poincaré, before going into the general session at noon. An emotional Pétain spoke of moving 24 divisions to the Amiens area (it was 15 the day before) and the British running away like the Italians at Caporetto. This enraged even the francophile General Wilson (CIGS). When an angry Foch intervened, Haig

▲ The Doullens Conference, 26 March. Field Marshal Haig is with the equally indomitably moustached Georges Clemenceau, the Prime Minister of France. The other civilian is M. Louis Loucheur, French Minister of Munitions, who worked effectively with his British counterpart, Winston Churchill.

offered to serve under his direction. The ten politicians and generals round the table eventually agreed that Ludendorff's advance must be stopped east of Amiens. At Haig's prompting, a Franco-British agreement was signed, giving Foch co-ordination not just of the immediate battle but of the entire Western Front and all Allied forces. By 4 p.m. Foch was seeing Gough, the unlucky absentee, breathing exhortations for his army to hold on east of Amiens. He also ordered General Fayolle to defend the ground 'foot by foot' – but this was liberally interpreted.

Ludendorff was feeling the strain of his six-day old battle, losing his temper around 7 p.m. on the telephone with Crown Prince Rupprecht and threatening to sack Below's chief of staff in disappointment at Seventeenth Army's progress. His ambitious evening orders directed Seventeenth Army on Abbeville–Doullens–St Pol; Second Army was to capture Amiens and reach the line Moreuil–Airaines (17 miles, west-north-west of Amiens); and Eighteenth Army was to advance against the French over the Roye–Avre river line towards Tartigny – Compiègne on the Aisne, supported by Seventh Army. These were widely divergent objectives even if the battered Seventeenth Army was to have the help of the separate 'Mars' attack towards Arras.

27 March: The French lose Montdidier

Ludendorff's soldiers were faltering from plain exhaustion against dogged defence. Their own rations were 48 hours in arrears as priority traffic carried ammunition across the tortured ground of the old Somme battlescape. Many knew the ground only too well from 1916 and devastating it the next year. Little wonder then that the very spoils of victory were beginning to intoxicate and delay the advance. The apparent victors could see that the allegedly U-boat starved British lacked for nothing in food, drink, or equipment. Waterproofs and boots were especially prized acquisitions.

Meanwhile, the British were falling back on ever richer depots and, despite estimated losses of 74,651 (over half of these on 21 March), nearer reinforcements and replacements. The regular 5th Division was arriving from Italy and, more significantly, the four strong élite Anzac divisions, some coming up in London buses from Doullens, were on hand to stiffen the line from Arras. Replacements including leave men were now pouring across the Channel at the rate of 10,000 per day. The War Cabinet had lowered the minimum overseas age limit by six months to 18½ after three months' training to find 50,000 conscripts, and released 611,000 men from munitions and agriculture.

All of this could have little effect on Fayolle's battle in the south. The French faced thirteen of Hutier's divisions including four rested ones and ample artillery, with only ten divisions in line (two cavalry), although another six were coming up. The pattern of the 26th was repeated. Gamelin's group, deployed in depth along the Divette, nullified all Generalleutnant Conta's attacks with 80 massed guns and the infantry enjoying a good field of fire.

Robillot's Corps and the new VI Corps were again the weak links. Their dismounted cavalry, cyclists and armoured cars fought desperately to hold gaps left by the ill-supplied infantry and buy time for 38th and 70th Divisions to come up, but from 10 a.m. a general retreat began. It ended after nightfall up to 7½ miles back with Robillot holding a line across the village-dotted watershed of the Avre and Matz south of Montdidier. This road/rail centre was entered by the German 206th Division around 9.30 p.m. The new French divisions relieved the cavalry although the indefatigable 5th Cavalry Division, despite its 50 per cent losses, found a battalion to extend 56th Division's precarious line west of the Avre. The 22nd Division had only about 30 per cent of its infantry left, and these men were not reformed until the 29th.

Fayolle chafed at being tugged between the priorities of covering Amiens before Noyon, urged by the visiting Foch, or of covering Noyon before Amiens, according to Pétain on the telephone. At all events, he determinedly urged on his reserves. Debeney's and Général de Division Marie de Mitry's headquarters south-west of Montdidier stayed put in the nine-mile gap between them and Humbert, although no troops covered the Montdidier road until 3 a.m. on the 28th.

The unreinforced Gough's line was still almost as long as Fayolle's and held by nine skeleton divisions against fifteen German of which just six had been first line on the 21st. Maxse's XVIII 'Corps', gradually getting its guns back from the French, only gave way up to a mile after its allies. The 108th Brigade's Irish Fusiliers dwindled to about 200. Counter-attacks actually took 371 prisoners from two of the finest German divisions. By midnight General Mesple's arriving 133rd Division and 4th Cavalry Division had relieved most of Maxse's survivors. In just a week they had lost 21,705 comrades.

Watts' extremely thin ranks were heartened by the centralized roar of 385 guns in what was later designated the virtually forgotten but epic Battle of Rosières. The field guns stayed in action when German infantry were only 600 yards away. The 8th and 24th Divisions were attacked about 7.30 a.m. by Lüttwitz's III Corps. Rouvroy was lost and recovered, only to be lost again around 2 p.m. when grenades ran out and Maxse's retreat uncovered the flank. In front of Rosières the defenders gave no ground despite waves of attacks literally drummed in. In the north by the Somme, 16th Division, already having suffered 5,543 casualties, fought for 4½ hours against converging German Guards' attacks before retreating two miles from Proyart to Morcourt. Somehow Watts and Heneker marched 300 troops five miles from the centre to launch a 2 p.m. counter-attack that retook the Harbonnières–Proyart crossroads and 217 prisoners. An hour later Brigadier-General E.P. Riddell on an artillery horse led every last man into a dramatic charge at Harbonnières from 300 yards against the German 208th Division advancing in eight to ten waves. The blow recaptured Vauvillers and restored 50th Division's front although renewed pressure and ammunition shortages later forced the British back to their light railway start line. Watts' men had taken 800 prisoners, far more than they had lost.

Generalmajor von Brauchitsch's brilliant morning initiative threatened this whole embattled line with encirclement. Commanding the held-up infantry of 1st Division immediately north of the Somme at Morlancourt, von Brauchitsch ordered his 3rd Grenadier and 43rd Regiments to turn 90°

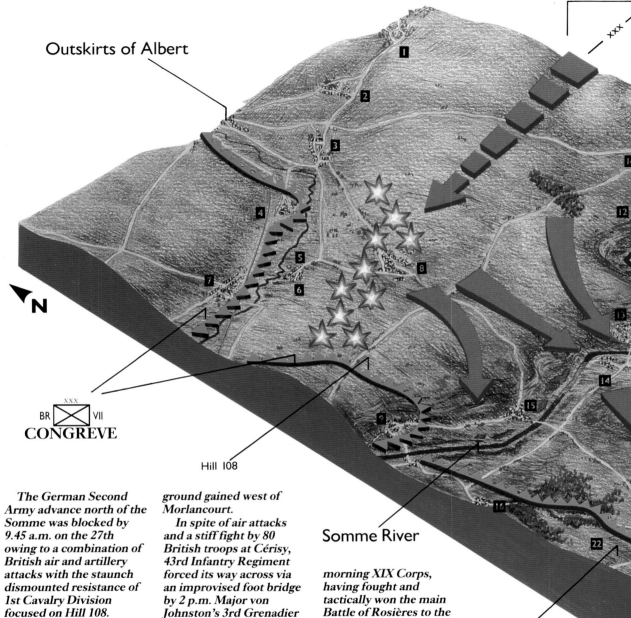

Outskirts of Albert

N

BR ⊠ VII
XXX
CONGREVE

Hill 108

Somme River

BR ⊠
X
CAREY'S FORCE

To Amiens
12 miles

Amiens
defense line

The German Second Army advance north of the Somme was blocked by 9.45 a.m. on the 27th owing to a combination of British air and artillery attacks with the staunch dismounted resistance of 1st Cavalry Division focused on Hill 108. Showing exceptionally prompt flexibility, Generalmajor von Brauchitsch telephone-ordered two of his infantry regiments of the 1st (Königsberg) Division to about-turn 90° to the left and cross the Somme at Chipilly-Cérisy to take the British Fifth Army south of the river in the rear. The 1st Grenadier Regiment would hold the ground gained west of Morlancourt.

In spite of air attacks and a stiff fight by 80 British troops at Cérisy, 43rd Infantry Regiment forced its way across via an improvised foot bridge by 2 p.m. Major von Johnston's 3rd Grenadier Regiment then reinforced the thrust, and its III Battalion captured the twin villages of Warfusée and Lamotte on the Roman Road by 7 p.m. between Fifth Army's two defence lines.

Although Johnston's troops were denied a farm west of Warfusée, the British response had been confused and disjointed, yet during the next morning XIX Corps, having fought and tactically won the main Battle of Rosières to the south, managed to escape obliquely across the front of the new German positions. Brauchitsch's superiors failed to exploit his success. In particular 4th Guard Division of the same XIV Corps did not know of the Cérisy success, and it may well be significant that Marwitz was moving forward his Army Headquarters that day.

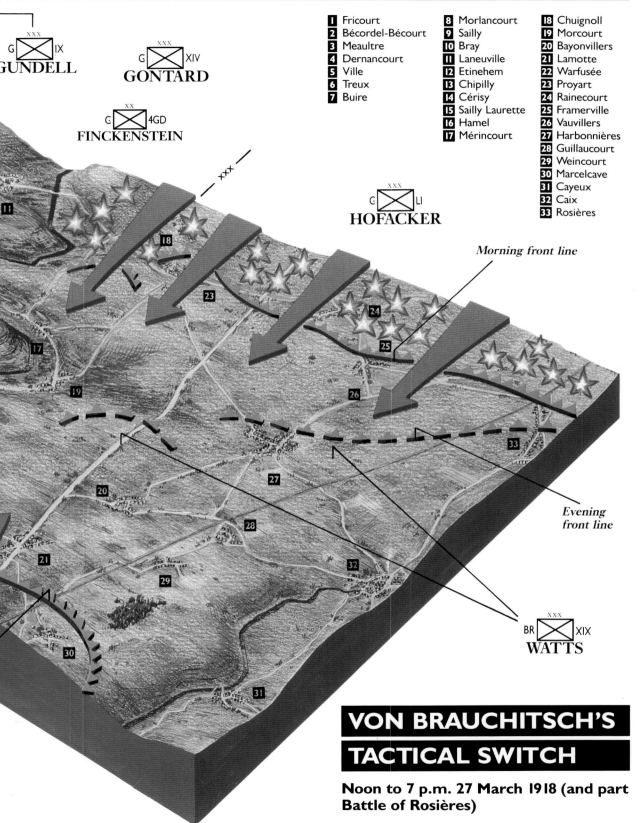

GUNDELL — G ⊠ IX

GONTARD — G ⊠ XIV

FINCKENSTEIN — G ⊠ 4GD

HOFACKER — G ⊠ LI

WATTS — BR ⊠ XIX

1 Fricourt
2 Bécordel-Bécourt
3 Meaultre
4 Dernancourt
5 Ville
6 Treux
7 Buire
8 Morlancourt
9 Sailly
10 Bray
11 Laneuville
12 Etinehem
13 Chipilly
14 Cérisy
15 Sailly Laurette
16 Hamel
17 Mérincourt
18 Chuignoll
19 Morcourt
20 Bayonvillers
21 Lamotte
22 Warfusée
23 Proyart
24 Rainecourt
25 Framerville
26 Vauvillers
27 Harbonnières
28 Guillaucourt
29 Weincourt
30 Marcelcave
31 Cayeux
32 Caix
33 Rosières

Morning front line

Evening front line

VON BRAUCHITSCH'S
TACTICAL SWITCH

Noon to 7 p.m. 27 March 1918 (and part Battle of Rosières)

south and cross the Somme opposite Cérisy. Despite air attacks, they planked the blown bridge and had captured the village by 2 p.m.

By 7 p.m., 3rd Grenadiers had captured the key Roman Road villages of Lamotte and Warfusée right on 16th and 39th Divisions' line of retreat to Carey's Force. Gough's response to the Cérisy crossing was to move 61st Division back in buses and lorries to Marcelcave behind Carey's Force, to be ready for counter-attack. Just before this order, around 5.30 p.m., Gough was told he would be relieved by General Sir Henry Rawlinson next day. It was a hard fate after conducting a skilful week-long fighting retreat on a scale without precedent in the history of the British Army.

Byng's Third Army recovered its poise, losing minor ground only in four places despite nineteen divisions assaulting its twelve. About 400 dismounted Dragoon Guards firmly held Sailly-Laurette in the Ancre–Somme peninsula until relieved by Major-General Sir John Monash's 3rd Australian Division. Around Albert, V Corps gave way along a two-mile stretch but counter-attacks made sure the high ground was retained. In the

town itself a German lorry-mounted 88mm flak gun demolished a British-held factory strongpoint and then shot down a Bristol fighter.

The Anzac-held Hébuterne re-entrant lay on the Below–Marwitz Army boundary, which meant attacks were poorly synchronized. Only 3rd Guard Division mortared and grenaded itself into Rossignol Wood to claim most of the 200 British prisoners lost by IV Corps and occupy two broken-down tanks. VI Corps also smashed the early attacks with machine-guns and artillery; 31st Division was levered back 2,000 yards by six hours' infantry infiltration attacks that reduced one defending battalion to 44 all ranks, but Lieutenant-General Haldane had his Guards in support and reinforced them with the 32nd Division's leading brigade.

▼ *The Germans display eight typical BEF types after their capture of Albert, 27 March. All seem to have lost their cap badges, no doubt as souvenirs of war. The group includes some Royal Artillery drivers (one in leather jerkin), a kilted (Gordon) Highlander with a wound stripe on his left sleeve, two other Scottish soldiers in bonnets, and a Tank Corps soldier second from the right. (IWM Q55248)*

Remote though he was, Crown Prince Rupprecht could read a failing battle. Early in the afternoon he ordered three reserve divisions to march and renew the crucial attack at Hébuterne. Ludendorff brusquely countermanded his army group commander and directed the troops south of the Somme towards Montdidier. The Bavarian retorted: 'Then we shall have lost the war!'

In the air, Third Army was again considerably aided by RFC ground attacks now concentrated on both sides of the Somme – to the tune of a record 50 tons of bombs and 313,345 bullets. Marching German columns particularly suffered. Aerial combat was intense over Albert, Richthofen scoring three victories (of his unit's 13), while the Canadian Second Lieutenant A. A. McLeod who won a Victoria Cross for repelling three Fokker triplanes and saving his wounded observer. German 'Battle Flights' struck four villages on the Ancre and on the Somme. The Germans admitted loss was three aircraft to 29 British.

28 March: The 'Mars' Turning Point

The day before, Foch had urged Pétain: 'not a metre more of French soil must be lost!' Today, Fayolle's army group for the first time showed it was ready to fight more than just a delaying action. Humbert's Third Army lost only one village to Generalleutnant von Werern's XVII Corps morning attacks and struck back at 1 p.m. with three divisions and up to 180 supporting guns. Three villages were stormed and, although the German 10th Division retook two, the moral victory and a gain of two miles went to the French. De Mitry's VI Corps retook three villages west of Montdidier from the surprised German 9th Division.

Von Hutier's army was reorganizing on the achieved Montdidier–Noyon line; only its two right wing corps were required to extend the Avre line to Moreuil. After a 90-minute bombardment, three divisions attacked the barely established Groupement Mesple and drove it back five miles through four successive positions to the line La Neuville–Aubercourt. Nevertheless, most of British XVIII Corps' survivors were relieved in the process.

Watts' XIX Corps in the Rosières pocket received orders to withdraw only at 4.45 a.m.. Three of its divisional commanders had met at midnight, warning of the danger of being cut off if Lamotte were not retaken. Watts was telephoned, and he rang Gough to get Foch's hold-fast order rescinded. At 3 a. m. the Fifth Army commander's call roused the Generalissimo from his bed and obtained permission to pull XIX Corps back to Carey's Force. The delay meant a confused daylight retreat to the south-west that cost the rearguard its brigadier-general's freedom. By midday the five 'divisions' had swung back coherently parallel to the upper Luce stream despite enfilade fire.

At noon 61st Division's 2,400-strong counter-attack, supported by 34 guns, began; but, over open ground, it could get no closer than 200 yards to 1st Division's villages on the Roman Road. The effort was abandoned within four hours. Groupement Mesple's retirement again exposed XIX Corps, whose afternoon retreat benefited from a rain squall and the cover of six Canadian armoured cars, although 8th Division lost most of two battalions owing to orders not getting through. Meanwhile Carey's Force, now 4,000 strong, with 1st Cavalry Division on its left, repulsed the first major attack it had to face. Its renewal by German Guards, however, after heavy shelling of Marcelcave, found that village empty. Carey's Force, stiffened by all the Corps signals company except Watts' last telephone operator, had dug in half-a-mile to the west.

The survivors of XIX Corps, covered by 39th Division's two battalions of infantry at Cayeux, fell back through the night across-country as well as via congested roads. Two divisions crossed each other's routes and, out of touch, marched across the Avre and partially even the Noye. They were now to rest in reserve as 20th Division's 1,000 reformed infantry came into line south of Carey's Force and the French 163rd Division came up by lorry.

Rawlinson took over command from Gough at 4.30 p.m., and the two generals conferred for an hour. The new Army Commander inherited just six divisions (one cavalry) in line, although two divisions of III Corps and the two other cavalry

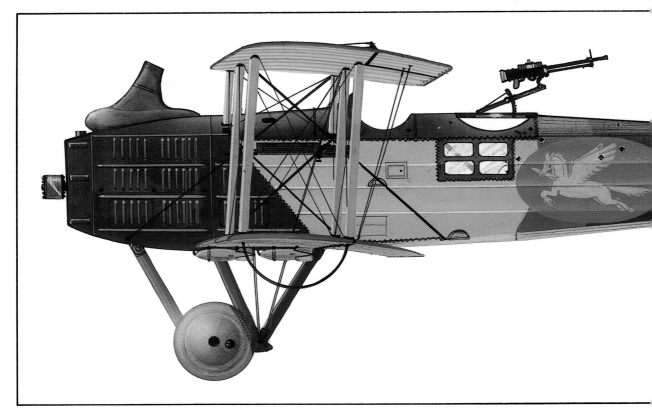

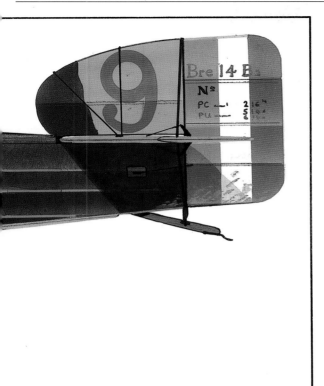

◀ *The French Breguet 14B2 two-seater biplane bomber flew operationally from the summer of 1917, over 2,000 being ordered. This robust Louis Breguet design had welded steel fittings and tail surface tubing. Its 12-cylinder Renault 300hp engine in a big cowling gave a top speed of 98mph at 10,000ft, which was reached in 11½ minutes. Defensive armament was a single Vickers machine-gun firing forward atop the fuselage (sometimes a Lewis gun added to or replaced this), and the observer had a twin ring-mounted Lewis with an optional rearward/downward-firing single Lewis as well. Armour was added to the pilot's cockpit and seat. The bomb rack could carry 32 8kg (17.61b) bombs or fewer heavier types. A fuselage side window and underside trapdoors assisted bomb aiming. The Breguet 14 equipped 71 French escadrilles and dropped almost 1,900 tonnes of bombs on the Western Front in 1918.*

◀ *A battery of British Third Army 18-pounder field guns in action west of Albert on 28 March. Freshly dug earth can be seen by the gun trail spades. These guns have already fired shells and are part of the lethal artillery support in the Ancre sector that day. Third Army began with 495 pieces and the BEF 2,887 (2 March); such weapons expended 5,471,489 shells 17 March-7 April. The Germans captured no fewer than 524 18-pounders up to 7 July. The 18-pounder had a range of 7,000 yards (nearly 4 miles), a maximum firing elevation of 6° and could fire eight rounds a minute. A column of infantry is visible beyond the battery's left flank. (IWM Q8655)*

divisions were marching from points 11–30 miles south of Montdidier to rejoin the meagre British line east of Amiens. Rawlinson rapidly wrote to Foch expressing his fears for the city if fresh troops did not arrive within 48 hours.

Third Army faced attacks by 29 of Rupprecht's divisions along the whole 33 miles from the Somme to Arleux, north of Arras. Marwitz's 3 a.m. telegrams failed to postpone Kathen and Watter's attacks north and south of Albert. Around Dernancourt the Australians wiped out 200 early morning infiltrators and, with 35th Division, repulsed three attacks. Between the Somme and Ancre, 3rd Australian Division (300 casualties) regained 600–1,200 yards in a late afternoon push for Morlancourt. At Aveluy Wood, 54th Reserve Division's Württembergers were crushed by fire and counter-attack in their efforts to expand the bridgehead over the Ancre against V Corps.

Harper's Anzac-stiffened IV Corps held the Hébuterne re-entrant, four divisions against nine. The only German gains were fractional, west of Rossignol Wood. The Anzacs actually extended their defences slightly by counter-attacks. Haldane's mainly Guards VI Corps bloodily repulsed five attacks by three of Below's divisions, although the defenders suffered from machine-guns, patrols and snipers.

Byng's troops had simultaneously won an old-fashioned day's victory. Ludendorff's long-matured 'Mars' sub-offensive pitted nine fresh divisions against four holding the strong and previously unassailed Arras bulwark. The 4½-hour bombardment began with mustard gas at 3 a.m. Though similar to that on 21 March, Bruchmüller had had no hand in this barrage. Another difference was the last-minute aerial strafing run before the infantry attacked at 7.30 a.m. without the benefit of screening fog and often shoulder to shoulder. By 5 p.m. the offensive had ground to a bloody halt with appalling losses, on both sides of the Scarpe. Nowhere had it penetrated more than two miles, the regular or Scottish defenders falling back only to the strong Green Line south of the river and to the front of the Battle Zone on the north bank.

Deep machine-gun team dugouts and uncut wire had sustained the Forward Zone's resistance. The British artillery was not neutralized as on the 21st; its guns fired 650-750 shells apiece, often at 300-600 yards. Vimy Ridge offered magnificent observation, and all German guns brought forward were silenced.

RFC artillery calls and low-level flying played their part on both sides of the Somme. Most of the 58 aircraft lost (German claim 31) fell to ground fire, but seven German machines were

destroyed. German artillery horses suffered particularly from air attack.

Ludendorff's total disappointment was expressed by evening orders halting 'Mars' and cancelling its 'Valkyrie' northern extension. Below was to transfer two divisions to Marwitz, who was belatedly ordered to capture Amiens by the shortest route, while Hutier's drive would resume on the 30th. No new offensive against the BEF alone was to be launched until 'Georgette' in eight to ten days' time.

29 March: The Battle of the Avre

A dark and storm-clouded Good Friday followed a bitterly cold and rainy night. It was to be the most uneventful day of Kaiserschlacht so far. Humbert's Third Army continued the previous day's local attacks, but the three divisions involved lost most of their morning gains to German afternoon counter-attacks from the woods between Onvillers and Boulogne la Grasse. Hutier was not distracted from attacking with ten divisions of his two right-hand corps against Groupement Mesple; Lüttwitz's Corps got three extra divisions for this

◀ *Royal Flying Corps pilots make reconnaissance reports to their CO near Albert, 25 March. The seated officer is Major H. V. Stammers of No 15 Squadron. His was a two-seater RE8 unit (up to 19 aircraft) supporting V Corps in the Flesquières salient from Lechelle airfield, the most forward air deployment in Third Army sector on 21 March as part of 12th (Corps) Wing in III Brigade. No 15 reported the German advance west of Bullecourt on the 21st and then, like many squadrons, had to move west, giving up airfields in the next week. The RE8 or 'Harry Tate' (after a contemporary music-hall star) was a stable if slow and vulnerable artillery spotting and reconnaissance workhorse.*

afternoon task. These, including the hitherto uncommitted 1st Guard Division, and Marwitz's southernmost 243rd Division, drove the French and their British supports (five battalions of 20th Division) back up to two miles on a seven-mile front between the Avre and the Luce, gaining Moreuil Wood.

De Mitry's VI Corps attack at 6 p.m. astride the Avre north of Montdidier ended in yielding a similar distance. Nevertheless First Army, despite the two indentations driven into its line, could count on five reinforcing divisions within 24 hours. This was partly why Foch, who had met Haig at Abbeville in the morning, could not relieve Fifth Army. Fortunately, for the first time, that British

formation was unattacked on its main line, although two divisional commanders fell victim to shelling. Regular cavalry and two hastily remounted yeomanry regiments reinforced Carey's Force, while III Corps' formations neared Amiens, and engineers began a reserve line through Gentelles.

North of the Somme trench warfare conditions had returned, with gas shelling from the German side. Ludendorff's afternoon orders, amplified by telephone at 6 p.m., stressed the importance of Marwitz's and Hutier's advancing to reach the road south of Amiens on a broad front 1½ miles west of the Noye. Three more of Below's divisions were to join the reserves backing this effort. It did not bode well for the High Command's plans that Marwitz's tired troops had hardly fought south of the Somme that day.

The BEF's recovered balance was perhaps best symbolized by the King's visits to GHQ and Third Army (once again Fifth Army was ignored by VIP visitors). Ironically, a royal cousin, the Kaiser, was simultaneously being optimistically briefed at Mons.

Fifth Army also got most of the day's weather-

▼ *German Eighteenth Army pioneers bridging a mine crater between St. Quentin and Ham, March 1918. Each divisional pioneer battalion generally had two companies of these troops. A medical unit (Bearer Company?) is marching by. The history of the*

German 247th Reserve Infantry Regiment, a zealous spearhead unit of 54th (Württemberg) Reserve Division, claims that such elderly labour troops were being slack around 29 March, saying they only had to work six hours a day. (IWM Q55241)

curtailed air support, to the tune of 259 bombs and strafing, mostly south of the Roman Road. The Germans lost two aircraft.

30 March: The Avre and Moreuil Wood

Fayolle now faced assault by Hutier's most successful German army on his entire 25-mile front from Noyon to Moreuil. The opening 90-minute barrage began at 7 a.m. heralding infantry attack by fourteen divisions. In the Noyon sector Gamelin's 9th Division found out H-hour from an order in a shot-down observation aircraft. This enabled V Corps artillery to pulverize the three German divisions forming up and to smash lorried reinforcements. After local French counter-attacks gained prisoners, fighting effectively ended before midday.

Once again Robillot's II Cavalry Corps, less cohesive and not so terrain-favoured, gave ground to the extent that generals themselves rounded up infantry stragglers. The French 1st Cavalry Division blocked gaps with its dismounted units, horse holders, cyclists and armoured cars. By noon, Robillot had rallied his troops 2,000-3,000 yards to the south with 67th Division coming up in relief.

The neighbouring (XXXV) Corps fell back less and kept its flank anchored to the Avre at Ayencourt.

Debeney's troops had a much more precarious battle west of Montdidier on a 10-mile S-shaped front. Only one of the four defending infantry divisions had its full nine battalions, and once more the dismounted dragoons, cuirassiers and hussars proved the stoutest defenders. Their counter-attacks gained prisoners and machine-guns, notably 16th Dragoons' mile-deep evening thrust to recapture le Montchel from 9th (Silesian) Division on the key Avre Army boundary. The 56th Division's commander described the crews of two participating armoured cars as 'several times heroic'.

Nevertheless the German offensive roughly doubled the Avre bridgehead. One of six villages taken was Cantigny, which the Americans would recapture two months later in their first major Western Front attack. In particular Lüttwitz's Corps had driven a dangerous bulge into the French XXXVI Corps sector south of Moreuil.

Fifth Army's fragments, supported by 69 heavy guns, withstood eight of Marwitz's divisions on an eight-mile front. The fresh 228th broke itself

against the northern Hamel sector suffering more than 700 killed and wounded. Carey's Force and the cavalry proved unshakeable. Only between the railway and Moreuil did the British line give. At Moreuil Wood, right on the Allied boundary, an Anglo-French air- and machine-gun-supported Canadian Cavalry Brigade (1,400 strong) attacked the wood at 9.30 a.m. on two sides. Four mounted and two dismounted squadrons cleared half the wood in a costly 90-minute mêlée. The other brigade of 2nd Cavalry Division followed and nightfall found 8th Division infantry sharing the undergrowth with seven depleted German battalions from three divisions.

▶ *A private/Lewis gunner of 17th Battalion, the King's Royal Rifle Corps (KRRC), 117th Brigade, 39th Division (New Army), a reserve formation for Fifth Army's VII Corps sector, in action from the 21st. The 17th KRRC, alone in the brigade Green Line sector on the 23rd, repulsed a German XXIII Reserve Corps dawn attack, enabling the whole brigade to retreat unharassed. From 4 a.m. on the 25th the unit was part of XIX Corps fighting in the Battle of Rosières and sharing in a 500-yard counter-attack near Demuin on 30 March. The 251b American-designed Lewis gun was air-cooled and fired up to about eleven 47-round .303in bullet pans a minute. Each battalion had 36 such weapons, or two per platoon plus four for anti-aircraft work.*

◀ *Canadian Cavalry Brigade horses killed during the successful but costly charge into Moreuil Wood on 30 March. The photograph was taken on 3 April, and rifle pits have been dug either side of the track. (IWM Q10858)*

Northwards, Rifle and Little Woods, named after their defenders, changed hands three times before 20th and 50th Division troops, shot in by 48 field and heavy guns, restored the morning line after 7 p.m.. North of the Luce 66th Division was helped by three 39th Division counter-attacks but Demuin eventually fell. Watts sent in 12th Lancers who retook a wood that became Lancer Wood. The similarly-committed 9th Australian Brigade (200 casualties) counter-attack could only regain another 200 yards from the Hanoverian 19th and Guard Ersatz Divisions. They had captured about a mile of ground and were 11 miles from Amiens.

Overnight Watts relieved three of his skeleton 'divisions' with about 1,800 infantry of the relatively rested 18th Division. North of the Somme, Byng's troops now clearly held the initiative. Monash's Australians repulsed three afternoon attacks and enfiladed 228th Division south of the Somme. The New Zealanders methodically advanced about 500 yards, inflicting 480 casualties and taking 125 machine-guns and mortars. The Guards crushed a 234th Division morning assault despite a 2¾–hour barrage and fourteen bombing aircraft. Third Army now had the Australian and Canadian Corps firmly holding either end of its line.

Haig lunched with Clemenceau at Fifth Army Headquarters and secured his promise that Debeney would recross the Avre and hold the high ground. Foch's *General Directive No 1* stipulated covering Amiens with present forces and forming reserve masses of manoeuvre north of it (British) and north of Beauvais (French). To the latter, Pétain accordingly directed 20 divisions including four from Italy (recalled 24-6 March).

31 March: Equilibrium

Easter Day, the pious Fayolle had recorded on the 29th, would save his army group. And indeed it was given, that Sunday, a showery morning with sunny intervals, further to consolidate its line of fourteen divisions against Hutier's twelve, except for German shelling from 7 a.m. From midday four French villages in Debeney's sector suffered local attacks. The most serious was 1st Prussian Guard Division's assault on Grivesnes which reached its château, only 5½ miles from Hutier's River Noye line objective. At that moment two

◀A British heavy artillery battery retreating, March 1918. The 5.2-ton gun is a Mark II 60-pounder. The urgency of the situation can be seen by the heavy Clydesdale shire horses breaking into a trot and the Royal Garrison Artillery crew riding the gear-laden gun's foot-rests.

French armoured cars drove in and routed these élite troops.

At noon Robillot's four infantry divisions with 108 '75s' and '155s' in support made careful limited advances, capturing tactical features by 5 p.m. from the opposing four divisions west of the Matz. Significant action also flared in the hitherto stalemated Oise sector of French Sixth Army. Around 5.30 p.m. at Chauny, Hessians of a regiment from the 75th Reserve Division (newly arrived from south of Laon) crossed the river on rafts. They all fell victim to 16th Entrenching Battalion of the British 58th Division.

Von Hofacker's LI Corps directed the day's *Schwerpunkt* between the Luce and Moreuil with an hour's softening up before 1 p.m. In two hours it took all three of the previous day's contested woods, thanks largely to the resilient 243rd Division and the 199th, a rested attack division. The tattered Allied line was then hardened by 2nd Cavalry Division's mounted brigades galloping up and a battalion of the new French 29th Division, as well as 200 8th Division survivors regaining the Moreuil Wood's separate north-west corner. Hofacker's men had made the only gain visible on Fayolle's situation map, of 2,000 yards

North of the Somme the only non-shelling action involved V Corps making a poorly synchronized and unsuccessful battalion attack west of Aveluy, which cost two of the four supporting Whippet tanks, and a brigade of 4th Division, recapturing 400 yards of trenches south of the Scarpe.

For the first time since the 25th, the RFC's last orders had emphasized high-level bombing and seeking out enemy aircraft. In fact the day

▼ German railway construction troops lay broad-gauge sleepers across the still-misty Somme battlefield, April 1918. Thick British wire entanglements can be seen on the right. Lack of repaired or new railway communication in the newly conquered British Fifth Army area by 30 March caused Ludendorff to postpone his final bid for Amiens for several days until sufficient track *had been laid to supply the offensive with artillery ammunition. The German Army Railway Service (made independent from Communication Troops in December 1916) had construction, traffic and store companies, with fourteen work and supplementary battalions. An Army Railway representative was in charge of movements and repairs in each corps area. (IWM Q55293)*

yielded but three Anglo-German aerial combats, so the fighters returned to strafing in the afternoon. Soon after 2.15 p.m. a III Corps squadron observer brought down fire that broke up 2,000 German infantry assembling to attack south of Moreuil. British night bombers dropped 628 bombs during a period of ten hours on German village billets and transport.

Total German air strength was now 822, 102 aircraft more than on the 21st, owing mainly to 76 additional fighters assigned to the Kaiserschlacht armies. Their opponents totalled 645 machines, but the French contribution certainly evened the odds. The Germans admitted four losses to 19 Allied.

After a midday conference at St. Quentin, Ludendorff cabled both his army group commanders that Marwitz's and Hutier's inner flanks, to be strengthened by six divisions, must press forward for Amiens astride the Avre. This deliberate but limited offensive would be delivered on 4 April, the earliest that logistics permitted, a notable factor being Second Army's ammunition shortage. Rupprecht himself, driving through the captured area between Péronne and Bapaume, saw the blocked road crossings and tired troops making 28-mile north-south marches that were the consequence of this redeployment.

1-3 April: A Relative Lull

The first three days of April represented a fighting though not a working lull for both sides. Fayolle's army group only had to repel small-scale attacks near Grivesnes and a night rush into Morisel (2/3 April). Pétain had now given his chief lieutenant 27 infantry and 5 cavalry divisions with 1,344 guns (528 heavy) and about 700 aircraft. In the south, Hutier's penetration had been sealed off in depth and, not surprisingly, both Foch and Fayolle were thinking of lancing the Montdidier bulge.

Debeney's sensitive junction with the British on the Avre had been strengthened. After Haig's representation to Clemenceau on the morning of the 1st about the Villers-Brettoneux plateau overlooking Amiens, Foch was summoned by telephone. Not long after 3 p.m. the Generalissimo agreed that the French should take over the three-mile sector from Moreuil (on the Avre) to Hangard (on the Luce). Over the next two nights the French 133rd and 29th Divisions finally and fully replaced Fifth Army's 8th and 14th Divisions.

Before this relief took place, that Army's seemingly indefatigable 2nd Cavalry Division had recaptured Rifle Wood using 1,000 dismounted troopers behind an eight-minute artillery preparation and with an overhead machine-gun barrage as well as air support from No. 84 Squadron. They took 100 German prisoners and thirteen machine-guns from the newly recommitted 25th Division, but counter-attacks raised the cavalrymen's losses to more than 300.

Third Army still faced 31 of Rupprecht's divisions in the front line with fifteen of its own, although six were extra-large Dominion formations. The Anzacs made local gains on the 1st, and the new 32nd Division from Ypres recaptured

▶ *A trooper of the Fort Garry Horse, Canadian Cavalry Brigade, 3rd Cavalry Division, Fifth Army. This regiment was in the second wave of the famous attack on Moreuil Wood (held by German 122nd Fusilier Regiment, 243rd Division), 30 March 1918. Losing one killed to shell-fire on the 21st, it had already been in a rearguard action on the 24th. Its CO, Lieutenant-Colonel R.W. Paterson, was commanding 3rd Cavalry Division's mixed mounted force then, and sent 6th Cavalry Brigade's detachment into its famous charge at Villeselve, the battle's other major mounted action.*

◀ *A German Army cinematographer films marching infantry on a road near Albert, April 1918. Surprisingly, Ludendorff had no cameramen filming Kaiserschlacht's opening day, but deploying cinematographic units elsewhere may have been part of his deception arrangements for the Allies. (IWM Q55252)*

Ayette from its 239th Division captors in a well-planned night attack, netting 192 prisoners with 20 mortars and machine-guns.

Foch also sent to GHQ his 1 April instructions to Fayolle on Anglo-French air cooperation, evidence that he had not ignored the third dimension of the battle. They laid down the axes of reconnaissances to ensure complete combined coverage; concentration of bombing on key rail junctions, notably St. Quentin, Jussy, Ham, Péronne; priority to ground attack and mutual reinforcement; and centralized dissemination of intelligence by radio,

◄ *A British Fifth Army 4.5in field howitzer on the road to Péronne, being passed by German transport and a 77mm field gun at the end of March 1918. Two British 18-pounder field guns have also been slewed to each side of the road. The howitzer's camouflaged gun shield, 45° elevation wheel, traversing lever and wheel brake shoes are all clearly apparent. This equipment weighed 3,004lb and fired a 35lb shell to 7,000 yards (4 miles) at up to four rounds a minute. The 4.5 formed one six-gun battery of the three in a standard Royal Field Artillery brigade (regiment). Third Army began with 164 such weapons; Fifth Army 288 (904 with BEF, 2 March). The British lost 154 field howitzers captured to Ludendorff by 7 July.*

◄ *Ragged, hungry infantrymen (German caption) eat every last morsel of their daily rations, having piled arms, during Eighteenth Army's Montdidier advance, at the end of March. From the shoulder-strap number, the unit seems to be the Rhine-recruited 81st Reserve Regiment of 222nd Division, a formation created north of Verdun in September 1916 and blooded on the Somme in November. In 1918 it was manning the Ailette (Aisne) sector until sent south-east of Montdidier, but it did not fight in Kaiserschlacht.*

courier aircraft, or daily motor vehicle to Foch's headquarters.

The first day and night of the RAF's existence saw no let-up in aerial activity. Fifth Army's six fighter squadrons flew all day, and its day bombers struck five villages as well as Péronne. Bapaume received three visits. Seventeen FE2b night bombers were active both sides of the Somme. Forty aircraft were lost (German claim 31), twelve to ground fire, and ten German aircraft claimed (4 admitted).

The RAF claimed thirteen German aircraft shot down south of the Somme on its second and third days of existence. These machines were part of the unified strike and reconnaissance arm Ludendorff had enjoyed since October 1916. Rosières advanced landing ground was the focus of an hour's 60-aircraft mêlée on 2 April, a significant pointer to German ground intentions.

3 April: The Beauvais Conference

A week from Doullens, the Allied top brass met again to redefine Foch's powers, as he had requested this from Clemenceau. The 3 p.m. gathering at his Beauvais headquarters headed by 'the Tiger' and Lloyd George included the US Generals Pershing and Tasker Bliss. They gave Foch 'strategic direction of military operations', and the Generalissimo issued *General Directive No 2*. This envisaged a major renewed German offensive north of the Somme with only a minor one south of the river. Accordingly, the Allies should launch a simultaneous counter-offensive around Montdidier and astride the Somme pending the present BEF defensive stand on the line Albert–Arras.

4 April: The Avre and Villers-Bretonneux

Kaiserschlacht's final objective line showed how modest Ludendorff's aims had become. The line set, Grivesnes–Ailly-sur-Noye–Gentelles Wood–Blangy Tronville, did not embrace the city of Amiens, but merely put its bridges and rail junction triangle under long-range shell fire from 12,000-14,000 yards. Fifteen divisions (six fresh) were to attack seven Allied on a 15-mile front.

The German artillery, supplied with ammu-nition thanks to the recent efforts of 60 railway construction companies in the devastated area, opened fire at about 5.15 a.m. for 75 minutes with liberal helpings of gas shell. As on 21 March, the *Minenwerfer* joined in the final phase, this time for fifteen minutes. The infantry assault began at 6.30 a.m. in persistent rain. Nine miles of attacking troops from twelve divisions (five fresh) fell on Debeney's First Army's five left and centre divisions which were supported by 958 guns including well over 200 British from Fifth Army.

Three French divisions gave way to sheer weight of numbers fighting through woods up to two miles and losing Morisel, Castel and Mailly-Raineval. The northernmost, 29th Division, stood fast from Rifle Wood to Hangard village (retaken); neither did 127th Division yield at Grivesnes. By 4 p.m. Debeney's artillery and reserves, including three fresh divisions, had not only checked the onset with terrible losses, but were counter-attacking. The cautious army commander went back to his headquarters and at supper broke out the champagne. Fayolle arrived to say emphatically that 'from today the Boches are *fichu*'.

Watts' final XIX Corps deployment around Villers-Bretonneux had the virtue of depth. Behind 14th and 18th Divisions, with a brigade of 2,250 Australians in the centre and 6th Cavalry Brigade in immediate reserve, there was the Gentelles Line, three to five miles behind and manned mainly by 3rd Cavalry and 24th Divisions. The 2nd Cavalry Division was the long-stop before Amiens. About 320 guns (80 heavy) supported the six-mile front. On average they fired 500 rounds each in ten hours' firing, often stopping German attacks over open sights. The northernmost, over-taxed and over-tired 14th Division, fell or ran back two miles in four hours, about 500 stragglers being forcibly rallied by Australian posts south of the Somme. Two regiments of 228th Division had broken its line from the Roman Road halfway to Hamel despite initial losses from their own artillery. This penetration enabled 5th Foot Guard Regiment to capture Hamel with 300 prisoners by midday including a brigade staff.

Meanwhile 35th Australian Battalion had re-pulsed the new 9th Bavarian Reserve Division's

Weather: rain

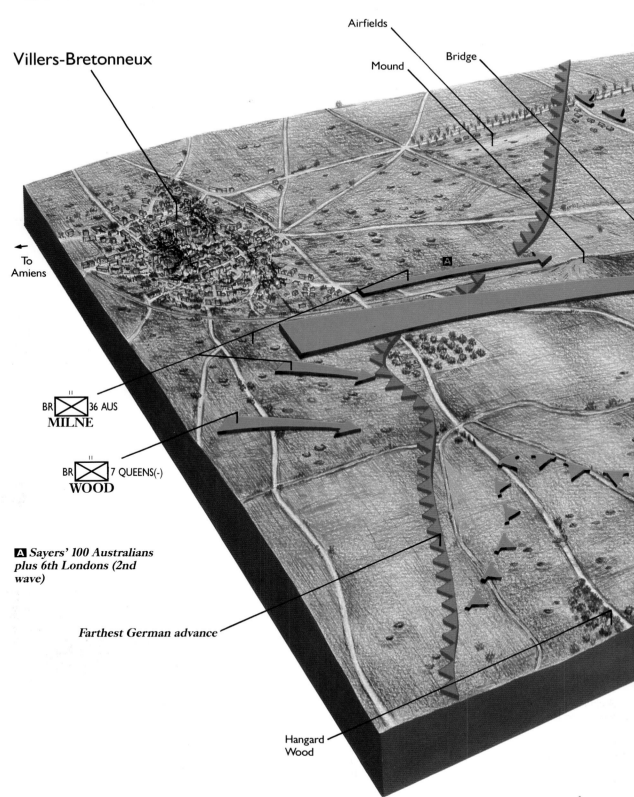

Airfields

Bridge

Mound

Villers-Bretonneux

← To
Amiens

A

BR ⊠ 36 AUS
MILNE

BR ⊠ 7 QUEENS(-)
WOOD

A *Sayers' 100 Australians
plus 6th Londons (2nd
wave)*

Farthest German advance

Hangard
Wood

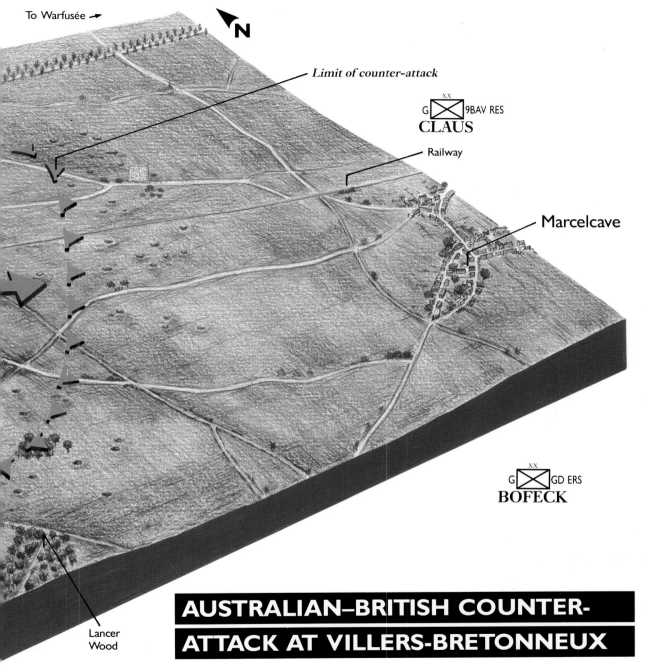

To Warfusée ➜

N

Limit of counter-attack

G ⊠ 9BAV RES
CLAUS

Railway

Marcelcave

G ⊠ GD ERS
BOFECK

Lancer
Wood

AUSTRALIAN–BRITISH COUNTER-ATTACK AT VILLERS-BRETONNEUX

5 to 6 p.m. 4 April 1918

A crucially timed, last-ditch Australian-led British counter-attack saved Villers-Bretonneux and the plateau above Amiens from imminent capture by the German

Second Army's 9th Bavarian Reserve Division advancing at 4.30 p.m. with all three infantry regiments (perhaps 5,000 men). The main German thrust was south of the

railway and Lieutenant-Colonel J. Milne (who was to be killed by a shell on 12 April) told his three company commanders of 36th Australian Battalion: 'Go till you're stopped and

hold on at all costs.' They did, despite 150 casualties, advancing over a mile beside the railway to the first bridge beyond Villers-Bretonneux.

three morning attacks and 18th Division three by Guard Ersatz and 19th Divisions. These units, partially uncovered by 14th Division's departure, fell back in the afternoon to trenches dug a mile east of Villers-Bretonneux. At this juncture Generalmajor Graf Finck von Finckenstein of 4th Guard Division suggested to his Corps commander, Generalleutnant von Gontard, that his reserve, the resourceful 1st Division, be committed to widen the breach. Gontard declined – a decision that may have cost Marwitz Villers-Bretonneux and more.

North of the Roman Road, 6th Cavalry Brigade rode up with 12 Hotchkiss machine-guns and reknit the 14th Division line on the high ground overlooking the town. Dismounted cavalry and artillery fire broke all Gontard's later attempts to continue the advance. South of the bisecting road, Kühne's XI Corps resumed its offensive after another hour's saturation shelling at 4 p.m. It was too much for 18th Division, which streamed back through rain and mud up to 2,500 yards to the Hangard Wood–Villers-Bretonneux road, except for its extreme flank which clung to the French in Hangard.

A gap opened to the north between the British

▲ The third infantry regiment of a German division (perhaps the 4th, from Pomerania) resting near Bapaume before an operation, in April. The ample ear and neck protection afforded by the 1916 pattern Stahlhelm is very clear.

and the now faltering Australians. Around 5 p.m. the Bavarians were within 440 yards of Villers-Bretonneux, and British batteries were withdrawing under fire. Then, from cellars in the town and positions outside, eleven weak Australian (about 600 men) and British (about 420 men) reserve companies, spearheaded by Lieutenant-Colonel J. Milne's 36th Australian Battalion, counter-attacked either side of the railway line to the east. Kühne's two divisions recoiled for up to 2,000 yards by 6 p.m.

North of the Roman Road, 17th Lancers cantered up to inspire 33rd Australian Battalion out of a mistaken retirement and link 6th Cavalry Brigade with the successful counter-attackers. Three Canadian motor machine-gun cars added their Vickers firepower against 9th Bavarian Reserve Division.

▶ *French cavalry and Renault autocanon reach a British-policed road junction, perhaps near Amiens late March or early April. The Renault autocanon armoured car had a Puteaux 37mm gun (the ordinary Renault having an 8mm Hotchkiss machine-gun) with a crew of three or four and a four-cylinder 4,600cc engine in an armoured lorry chassis. Robillot's II Cavalry Corps had seven armoured car groups of twelve vehicles each. They did sterling work holding up and then repelling Hutier's advances from 25 March.*

▶ *A strikingly posed German photograph. Two infantrymen have scooped sleeping space round the rim of a 1918 Somme shell-hole. The water in such craters was used for shaving, unless it had been polluted with mustard gas.*

By 7 p.m. the line had coalesced and an Australian night advance astride the railway even gained another 200-300 yards to reach their afternoon trench. The day and night cost 661 Australian casualties and 167 to 7th Cavalry Brigade. Two regiments alone of 4th Guard Division lost 498 all ranks.

The rain that made conditions on the ground a misery prevented any flying in the morning. V Brigade nevertheless made low-level attacks in the afternoon, and this pattern was repeated on both sides of the Somme during the 5th (200 bombs dropped and 20,000 rounds fired). German losses were four aircraft to five British).

5 April: The Final Push

Hutier's troops were too exhausted to renew the attacks. In particular, ammunition supply for the Avre bridgehead was precarious. Instead, five of Debeney's divisions counter-attacked the German line from Cantigny to Castel throughout the day. Little ground was recaptured, although a few French heavy tanks were used at Grivesnes, and Fayolle considered his troops capable of only limited trench warfare assaults. But a moral turning point had been reached.

The German Second Army effort was little better south of the Somme, despite Marwitz's orders to outflank Villers-Bretonneux on both sides. Kühne countermanded his half of the attack and did not recommit 24th Reserve (Saxon) Division. Gontard did order Hill 104's capture but, after an hour's shelling from 10 a.m., four regiments of 228th and the belatedly brought up 1st Division could get no farther than 150 yards from their start-lines. Australian and cavalry automatic fire with artillery support forced them to dig in and caused more than 208 casualties.

Byng's Third Army was on alert for its final ordeal, warned by prisoners of the previous night. The gas shelling began at 7 a.m. but proved patchy. Rupprecht's infantry went over the top two hours later. Against VII Corps' all-Australian-held lower Ancre sector, von Kathen's three divisions and 16,000 gas shells gained 1,000-1,500 yards north of Dernancourt.

Additional 3rd Jäger Assault Battalion Stostruppen had been used as well as single field guns against machine-gun nests (Ludendorff's 30 March general order), but a 4th Australian Division counter-attack by four battalions forced 50th Reserve Division off the key crest after 5.15 p.m. Kathen's troops lost 1,300-1,600 men against about 1,233 Australians, whose own active artillery expended 27,588 shells.

On the Albert–Hamel sector of the Ancre, V Corps successfully resisted four of Marwitz's divisions, whose net gains from twelve hours' fighting were an orchard and a few rifle-grenaded shell holes in Aveluy Wood. Below's left flank threw in six divisions against the Hébuterne re-entrant with the aim of capturing it and Colincamps (codename 'Loki') after four hours' shelling. All was pre-empted by a British 37th Division 5.30 a.m. effort to recapture Rossignol Wood. Two battalions had the lavish support of eleven tanks with 120 guns providing creeping barrage, smoke-screen and pinpoint suppressive fire. Only one unditched tank got into action, but the infantry advanced almost halfway through the wood before the general German attack forced them back.

Von Lindequist's XIV Reserve Corps did not break through the centre as planned. Instead the only meagre gains were on the re-entrant's shoulders, Le Signy Farm from the New Zealanders and the east half of Bucquoy from 42nd Division.

Both the German Army's supreme figures had eloquently succinct comments on the sixteenth and final day of Kaiserschlacht. Hindenburg wrote, 'our strength was exhausted', and Ludendorff, 'the enemy's resistance was beyond our powers'. In recognition of that, on the evening of the 5th he ordered attacks to stop.

▶The End of the Battle, 4/5 April 1918. Ludendorff's advance had achieved a maximum of 40 miles in sixteen days, notably between the St. Quentin area and the line attained astride the Avre north of Montdidier. These are impressive tactical gains on the map but achieved no strategic result, falling about 7½ miles short of Amiens at the closest point. Instead, Marwitz's and Hutier's Armies would be squeezed out of the Montdidier–Somme bulge by Allied counter-offensives in August. In the north, due east of Arras, Below's Army had gained only two miles and farther south had failed to envelop and drive Byng's Third Army north-west, away from its Arras hinge.

The End of the Battle, 4/5 April 1918

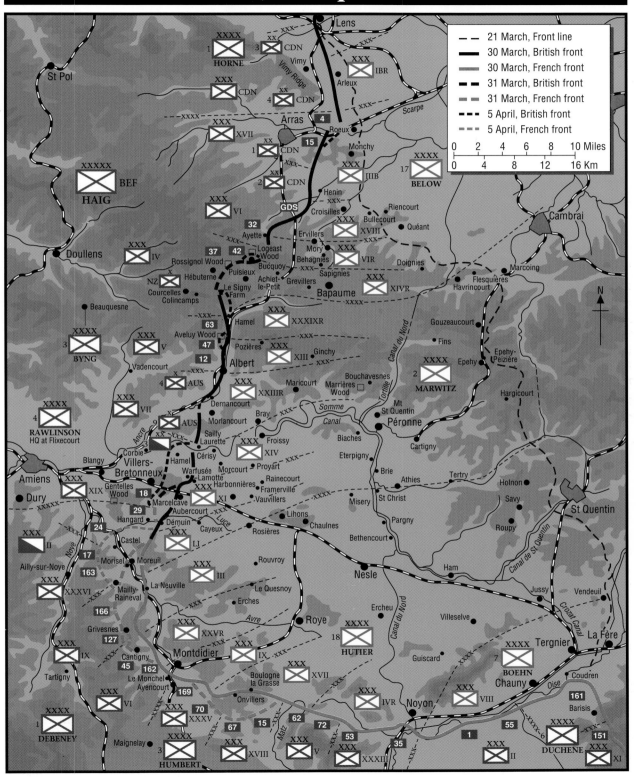

– – –	21 March, Front line
———	30 March, British front
▬▬▬	30 March, French front
– – –	31 March, British front
– – –	31 March, French front
····	5 April, British front
····	5 April, French front

0 2 4 6 8 10 Miles
0 4 8 12 16 Km

Lens
XXXX 1 · 3 CDN **HORNE**
Vimy
XXX IBR
XXX CDN
Arleux
4 XX CDN
Vimy Ridge
Scarpe
XXX XVII **Arras** 4
Roeux 15
Monchy
1 XX CDN
XXX IIIB 17 XXXX **BELOW**
2 XX CDN
Cambrai
XXX VI **GDS**
32
Henin
Riencourt
Croisilles
Bullecourt
Quéant
XXX XVIII
Ayette
37 42 Logeast Wood
Ervillers
Mory
Behagnies
Doignies
Marcoing
XXX IV **Doullens**
Rossignol Wood
Bucquoy
Sapignies
XXX VIR
NZ X **Hébuterne**
Puisieux
Achiet-le-Petit
Grevillers
Flesquières
Havrincourt
Courcelles
Le Signy Farm
Bapaume
XXX XIVR
Colincamps
Beauquesne
63
Hamel
XXX XXXIXR
Gouzeaucourt
XXXX 3 **BYNG**
47 Aveluy Wood
12
Pozières
XXX XIII
Ginchy
Fins
Epehy Peizière
Vadencourt
Albert
Maricourt
Marrières Wood
XXXX 2 **MARWITZ**
Epehy
4 XXX AUS
XXX XXIIIR
Bouchavesnes
Mt St Quentin
Hargicourt
XXX VII
Dernancourt
Bray
Somme
Tortille
Canal du Nord
RAWLINSON HQ at Flixecourt
9 XX AUS
Morlancourt
Canal
Biaches
Péronne
Sailly Laurette
XXX XIV
Froissy
Cartigny
Corbie
Cérisy
Villers-Bretonneux
Hamel
Morcourt
Proyart
Eterpigny
Brie
Athies
Tertry
Holnon
Amiens
XXX XIX
Warfusée
Lamotte
Raincourt
Framerville
St Christ
Savy
Dury
18 Gentelles Wood
Harbonnières
Vauvillers
Misery
St Quentin
29 Marcelcave
Aubercourt
Lihons
Pargny
Roupy
Hangard
Démuin
Cayeux
Chaulnes
Bethencourt
24
Castel
XXX LI
Rosières
XXX II
17 Morisel
Moreuil
Rouvroy
Ham
Nesle
Jussy
Vendeuil
Ailly-sur-Noye
163
Mailly-Raineval
La Neuville
XXX III
Le Quesnoy
XXX XXXVI
166
Erches
Ercheu
Villeselve
La Fère
Grivesnes
127
Roye
XXX XXVR
18 XXXX **HUTIER**
Tergnier
XXX IX
Cantigny
45 162
Boulogne la Grasse
XXX XVII
Guiscard
7 XXXX **BOEHN**
Montdidier
IX
Le Monchel Ayencourt
169
Onvillers
XXX IVR
VIII
Chauny
Coudren
Oise
161
XXX VI
70 XXXV
67 15 62 72
53
35
Noyon
Barisis
XXXX 1 **DEBENEY**
Maignelay
3 XXX XVIII **HUMBERT**
XXX V XXXIII
1 55
XXXX **DUCHENE**
XXX XI

BALANCE SHEET
AND AFTERMATH

By 4 April the BEF had received 101,000 infantry replacements, often eighteen-year-olds and younger. Its entire Cavalry Corps had fought in a manner reminiscent of the 1914 campaign, losing 4,300 of its mainly regular soldiers in a priceless display of mobility and solidity. Haig called them his best troops, while Gough and Rawlinson both took comfort from their presence in the line or in support. In a sense, and ironically, they compensated for a re-equipping Tank Corps that, because of tank and fuel losses, was able to do little in the second week except provide Lewis gun detachments on the Ancre. The value of mounted troops able to pick their way through the cratered fields, trenches and across the waterways of the Somme is also demonstrated by the fact that the French used no fewer than five divisions (two dismounted) to cover or bolster the concentration of Fayolle's Army Group. Theirs was no mere skirmishing role; incomplete March casualty figures for three of these formations total 2,265.

Allied Casualties

The British official history (1937) gives Haig's total loss as 177,739 men, of whom some 72,000 were prisoners, at least a third of them wounded or gassed. This was an average daily loss rate of over 11,000 men, and three times that of the 1916 Somme campaign. Gough's Fifth Army (including VII Corps for the duration) lost an estimated 90,882 men, and its sixteen infantry divisions were on average 50 per cent harder hit than Byng's 23 formations (total loss 78,860). Of the nine infantry corps engaged, Watts' XIX suffered the worst; more than 32,500, of whom 19,000 were missing. Two of its divisions (the 16th was one from the 25th) lost over 7,000 troops as did 36th (Ulster) Division in Maxse's Corps. Third Army's worst-hit division was the 59th with 6,038 casualties,

nearly two-thirds (807 killed) on the first day. Not one of Haig's original 30 infantry divisions lost fewer than 1,950 men, or about 20 per cent. Five Dominion divisions suffered 7,211 casualties in the ten days they were engaged. Even the 500 US 6th Engineers lost 77 officers and enlisted men.

French losses were about 77,000 from 20 divisions engaged, an indication of severe fighting. The March fighting alone cost three of Robillot's formations, 4,798 *poilus* hit or captured. Lundendorff claimed more than 90,000 Allied prisoners on 4 April, of which perhaps 13,000–18,000 were French.

Materially the Allies had lost 1,300 guns, the vast majority British; 2,000 British machine-guns captured (Ludendorff's Press claim by 27 March); about 200 tanks (all British); an unknown number of armoured cars; tens of thousands of horses; sixteen airfields; and over 400 British aircraft, not counting a substantial but unknown number of French machines. Left behind were 300 disabled locomotives and tractors; nearly 20,000 burnt-out railway wagons and thousands of tons of stores and ammunition. Fifth Army had blown up 248 bridges in its zone alone.

Yet most of these heavy material losses were soon replaced. On 26 March, Winston Churchill, Minister of Munitions, listed 1,915 guns that were being delivered to Haig by 6 April. The munitions factories worked without an Easter break. Machine-gun production was 10,000 a month. GHQ ordered 230 million rounds of small-arms ammunition on or before 26 March, this being nine per cent of the 1918 output. Tank production was over 100 a month. Within a month of Kaiserschlacht, RAF serviceable aircraft strength had risen by 276 to 1,310 and its overall trained pilots by 374 (9 March to 6 April). This was despite the highest weekly loss rate of the war, or more than 19 aircrew lost per 100 sorties during

▶*A German Seventeenth Army field dressing station near Arras in 1918. The site looks newly occupied and appallingly makeshift. Out of all Ludendorff's Kaiserschlacht preparations, the medical arrangements were the least successful. He complained that lightly wounded men hurried pell-mell to the rear. In fact an officer, NCO and soldier (of a machine-gun company) wounded in early April needed three days of walking and hitching lifts to reach St. Quentin. Even a Stosstruppen officer wounded on the second day had to find his own transport back. A flak gun commander has stated that horse-drawn forage wagons were commandeered at the last moment for casualty evacuation when losses exceeded expectations.*

▶*A dead British infantryman with his entrenching tool on the left. Some overhead cover has been improvised with corrugated sheeting behind a brick wall. BEF infantry strength on 1 March 1918 stood at 514,637, and by 31 March the Adjutant-General estimated infantry and cavalry casualties alone (the latter had heavier losses in April) at 124,462. (IWM Q23684)*

24-30 March, worse even than 'Bloody April' 1917. Forty-five new airfields had been laid out. The BEF received 111 standard locomotives and 2,042 wagons in April and May. American locomotives were also arriving to sustain the Allied railways which had laterally moved a record 46 divisions in 20 days.

Geographically, Kaiserschlacht had driven an enormous bulge of 1,200 square miles up to 40 miles deep into the Allied lines – more ground than the French and British had forcibly wrested from the invader in three years. Yet it contained no town or ground of strategic or industrial importance, and the prestigious prize of Amiens lay tantalizingly out of reach. The Allies still had two north–south railway lines to the west. The Western Front had been lengthened by about 26 miles and thirteen German divisions lay in an awkward shallow bridgehead over the Avre northwest of Montdidier. They were still appreciably east of the line reached in August 1914.

German Losses

These showy gains and trophies had cost the Kaiserschlacht armies the ghastly total of 239,000 men (1944 official history figure, to 10 April), an average daily blood sacrifice of 11,400 soldiers. Such intense attrition had not been seen since the gigantic head-on clashes of August 1914. Hutier's largest, Eighteenth, Army incurred 84,800 casualties from 35 divisions engaged, but they took 51,218 Allied prisoners in the first week. Marwitz's troops came off proportionately worse with 73,800 men removed from 24 divisions engaged. Below's Seventeen Army butcher's bill of 81,200 reflects its disappointing and costly push for Arras in which twelve divisions joined the original seventeen. As early as 30 March Rupprecht recorded his divisions' losses as 2,000-3,000 each. Tank and artillery losses are unavailable, but the admitted figure for the never all-out engaged air force is 76 aircraft lost.

Although Allied losses were slightly heavier in manpower with far more men lost permanently as prisoners, the qualitative loss was worse for the attackers. The *Stosstruppen* took heavy losses on 21 March and 4-5 April. One typical division, the 185th, second class in Allied classification, lost no fewer than 90 officers in the 28 March 'Mars' attack, i.e., more than half its infantry's commanders. NCO casualties were equally serious for the German Army. Immediate replacements came up in batches of 400-1,000 per division, but these could be 1919 class conscripts or returned wounded. Numerically, they did not substitute for the fallen, nor did they have their high morale and intensive training.

After Kaiserschlacht

Flattered by Kaiserschlacht's immense tactical gains, Ludendorff would attack four more times in the next four months. None of these later offensives matched Kaiserschlacht in scale or results, even the well-planned Aisne 'Blücher' attack against the French that regained the Marne 40 miles from Paris (27 May to 5 June). Another bulge was sealed off, this time by American, British and Italian troops as well as French. By mid-July, when Ludendorff still sought to deal the British the death-blow in Flanders that his small-scale April Lys or 'Georgette' attack had not been, the balance of forces had inexorably tipped against Imperial Germany.

Foch and Haig not only had massed tanks, gas and smoke shell for improved artillery fire, and superior overall numbers, but they also had a recovered British Army to be the cutting edge of the almost continuous Allied offensives of the last four months. Aiming the once-only Kaiserschlacht at Flanders in March or April might just have produced a breakthrough to Hazebrouck and the Channel ports, destroying the BEF's most vulnerable base area. Directing it south at the weak but resilient Fifth Army ensured massive intervention by French reserves, speeded up the 'Doughboy' influx across the Atlantic and frightened the Allies into a unity of command that brought them victory.

▶*The end of a British field artillery battery before Albert, March 1918. This unit, like several, left its withdrawal too late to avoid annihilating retaliatory fire. The ammunition limbers still look fairly full, and the horses remain harnessed. Kaiserschlacht had its untold thousands of animal casualties.*

CHRONOLOGY

28 July to 12 August 1914 Main European declarations of war.

5 to 9 September First Battle of the Marne ends German hope of rapid Western Front victory.

1915 to 1917 Trench warfare stalemate on Western Front.

23 October 1917 Ludendorff's operations chief writes appreciation of 1918 offensive in the West.

11 November Ludendorff convenes General Staff Conference at Mons to consider 1918 offensive in West.

20 November British surprise tank thrust at Cambrai.

30 November to 3 December Limited German counter-offensive in Cambrai sector wipes out British gains.

15 December Armistice of Brest Litovsk formally closes down Eastern (Russian) Front. Peace talks start on 22nd.

27 December Ludendorff's second council of war.

January to February 1918 German Army training and reinforcement (21 divisions) phase; BEF winter reorganization from 10 January (to 4 March).

21 January 1918 Ludendorff decides on Operation 'Michael' spring offensive option after tour of front. D-Day to be 14 March.

1-12 March German advance ground and air units deploy. Infantry begin to concentrate 6-12½ miles behind front. Crown Prince Rupprecht gets week's postponement of D-Day to 21st.

3 March Treaty of Brest Litovsk brings peace between Russia and Central Powers.

10 March Hindenburg issues 'Michael' operation order and final period of artillery preparation begins.

16-19 March 60 infantry divisions move up to front.

Yorck') offensive, Third Battle of the Aisne.

9-14 June Fourth Ludendorff ('Gneisenau') offensive, Battle of the Matz or Montdidier.

15-17 July Fifth Ludendorff ('Marne–Reims' or

20 March Ludendorff orders 'Michael' for 4.40 a.m. on 21st.

21 March KAISERSCHLACHT BEGINS: Operation 'Michael' (three armies with 65 divisions) smashes British Fifth Army and damages Third Army (maximum of 27 divisions) up to a depth of six miles for about equal losses on a front of 40 miles.

23 March General retreat of half the BEF to the Somme; Third Army abandons Péronne and Cambrai salient. First French troops engaged in south. German forces on both sides of Somme now ordered to split Allies. Crisis of battle.

24 March Allied command crisis begins. Byng's Third Army loses Bapaume; Gough's Fifth Army put under French command.

26 March BEF ordered to hold line of Somme with Anzac reserves reaching Third Army, but it loses Albert. At Doullens Conference, Foch becomes *de facto* Allied Generalissimo.

27 March French Third Army loses Montdidier, but Gough's surviving Fifth Army fights heroically to stem German Second Army.

28 March Widened German Seventeenth Army 'Mars' offensive on Arras (Third Army) sector fails in day. Gough replaced by Rawlinson. Ludendorff orders 'Georgette' for Flanders in eight to ten days' time.

30 March German Eighteenth Army presses for Amiens.

2 April British Fifth Army formally abolished (becomes Fourth Army).

4-5 April Last German push for Amiens halted about ten miles to east by exhaustion and a mainly Australian-stiffened British defence.

5 April KAISERSCHLACHT ENDS.

9-29 April Second Ludendorff ('Georgette') offensive, Battle of the Lys.

27 May to 4 June Third Ludendorff ('Blücher-*Friedensturm*') offensive, Second Battle of the Marne.

18 July to 11 November Allied 'Hundred Days' offensives lead to Armistice.

WARGAMING KAISERSCHLACHT

The First World War was a war in which commanders had remarkably little control over their troops once they had been committed to battle. When designing our wargame we need to be constantly aware of this factor. In fact, the period is remarkably suitable for wargaming because it allows genuine 'armchair' generalship! By putting our players, so far as possible, in the positions of a commander and his staff they will soon realise the necessity of drawing up detailed plans, trying to cater for every eventuality in advance, knowing that once the battle starts it will be very difficult to implement changes.

Given the significant delays in passing information up and down the chain of command, a particularly useful technique is the multi-layered game in which players take different roles at each layer. For example, three or four players might represent the commander and staff of a Corps. They plan their attack on maps and then hand all the details to an umpire, who compares it with a defence scheme drawn up either by himself or by another team. The two teams can then either compare their two schemes and talk through the likely outcomes. Or they can play another game, perhaps as a brigade staff, in which they have to execute the plan they have just produced from their château. This type of game can be very successful at showing just how difficult was the job of First World War planners, without radio or fast means of transport.

Board Games

Board games cannot strictly be regarded as simulations, since they give the players far too much information about both their own forces and those of the enemy. Nevertheless they are very useful at acquainting us with the broad geography of the campaign and the balance of forces involved. Two games about *Kaiserschlacht* have been published by Simulations Publications Inc (SPI); both are now out of production, but it should be possible to obtain them via the second-hand games market. The first was *1918*, which appeared in the early 1970s and used divisional level counters to depict the whole of the 'Michael' offensive. More recently, *Kaiserschlacht* depicted the Péronne–Ham crucial Fifth Army front down to brigade level.

Board games can also be used as the basis for Committee or Map games. The maps, orders of battle and rules can be used by an umpire, leaving the players free to discuss the situation, although this needs to be translated from the board game language. An example of this technique was used by Steve Badsey in his large wargame, or megagame, of *Kaiserschlacht* held at Sandhurst in 1981.

The Megagame employed more than thirty people to simulate the role of Gough's Fifth Army Headquarters in the first week of the offensive. About a dozen players represented Gough and his staff officers dealing with operations, intelligence, supply, medical and so on. From a classroom equipped with a large map they issued orders by telephone or 'pink' form to umpires who executed them on a large board game style map display. The umpires played the Germans and reported back to the Fifth Army players after an appropriate delay. Each hour represented one day, and so procedures were necessarily streamlined. Nevertheless this type of game exemplifies our definition – a model of the real thing designed to bring out the main points, in this case, emphasising command and control. This style of game can, of course, be played with fewer participants. A divisional attack can be played by, say, four players representing the Commander, Chief of Staff, Intelligence Officer and Artillery Commander; brigades by a player each; while a couple of umpires handle the higher and flanking units and the defenders.

Committee Games

The Mons Conference held on 11 November 1917 to discuss the objectives of *Kaiserschlacht* forms an ideal committee game for four players. There was no debate about *whether* an offensive was to be launched, but there were several alternative objectives. The conference was chaired by Ludendorff and attended by General von Kühl (Chief of Staff, Army Group Crown Prince), Colonel von der Schulenberg (Chief of Staff, Army Group Prince Rupprecht) and Lieutenant-Colonel Wetzell (Head of the Operations Section of the General Staff). Kühl favoured an attack on the Ypres salient; Schulenberg preferred Verdun as the main objective. Wetzell was happy with either but did not want Ludendorff's preferred choice – an ambitious assault at the boundary of the British and French armies. As *de facto* Supreme Commander, Ludendorff can, of course, take what option he wishes, but the German tradition of frank debate by Chiefs of Staff helps to produce a useful discussion of the options. If desired, some dramatic licence can be taken by creating characters to put forward other options such as the strategic *defensive* or, most uncharacteristically for the Second Reich, the political goals of Germany in 1918.

A similar game for the Allies could be designed around the Doullens Conference when Foch was appointed Supreme Commander. The front is cracking (as it did in May 1940) and the British are looking over their shoulders to the Channel ports; the French know they cannot hold the Germans alone and that the Americans will not be present in large numbers for months. Will the two sides sink their differences and combine their forces, or will they split apart to cover their respective capitals?

Background inspiration for both games can be found in *The Swordbearers* by Correlli Barnett and in his bibliography.

'Durchbruch' Bruchmüller

The massive German bombardment offers plenty of scope for a fascinating game about the artillery and intelligence aspects of *Kaiserschlacht*. During the winter, but particularly during March, each side would be trying to build up a picture of activity on the other side of the line. The British would want to identify the date and time of the offensive so that they could fire a counter-bombardment as the attackers crowd into their jump-off trenches; the Germans will try to identify as many targets as possible – defensive positions, artillery batteries, headquarters. In this game, each turn will last a day and will conclude when the offensive starts or the British fire their counter-bombardment – if they fire before the scheduled day, they can be regarded as having lost.

First, create a map outlining several divisional sectors along the front, and draw the three trench lines on each side. Each sector, on each side, will contain a number of targets – company positions, batteries, headquarters – and each will have a degree of protection and camouflage. Then mark on it those areas that can be observed from the ground on each side and, beyond them, the areas visible by balloon. Other areas can only be observed by aircraft. Each day the Germans will have to introduce new battery positions, dumps, shelters, roads, light railways and trenches into their front line. They can do this slowly (taking time over camouflage) and unobtrusively (not digging in visibly) or quickly but without taking trouble over protection. The rate of reinforcement will be such, though, that a degree of speed will be essential to meet the deadline.

In this game the players deploy their units to gather information about the enemy while at the same time trying to stop the other side gathering information about them. They will use aircraft for Offensive and Defensive Patrols, Photo-recce, Artillery observation and Balloon-busting. Artillery may Register targets before the offensive but may also dig in, camouflage itself, Move or bombard targets. The Infantry can Raid (with artillery support), Dig or Move. Finally the Logistics elements can Move reinforcements, Dig in or Camouflage units and Build installations such as dumps and roads. Rules will govern the number of dumps, positions and routes required for each division so that each player knows what he is looking for. Camouflaged targets will be difficult to see and dug-in ones hard to destroy, but they will take time to protect. As a guide, roads and trenches are dug first, dumps prepared and then infantry and artillery brought up behind the lines. Finally the artillery occupies its positions, during the last night or two before the attack, and the assault troops mass in their trenches. It is at this moment that they are most vulnerable to a counter-bombardment. Weather will occasionally affect observation and so hinder the efforts of both sides. Players will also try to deceive the enemy by constructing dummy positions or moving units to alternative locations just before the battle starts. Who will find out what he needs to know in time?

Der Tag

A fascinating game can be made about the events of 21 March itself. The aim of this game would be to see how the German assault tactics worked. First of all it is necessary to construct the defence system of a British division. We can either create our own using a modern 1:25,000 map or use an historical example from a divisional history or a contemporary trench map from the Imperial War Museum or the Western Front Association. A plan is then made to break through the system, either by an umpire or a player team representing German divisional or corps staffs. They need to assign targets to the artillery and objectives for the infantry regiments. The results of the artillery fire are assessed and then the fortunes of one or more German regiments can be followed as they fight their way through the British lines. To simulate the effects of the fog, each regiment should have to 'fight' its way up a long narrow table, on which successive terrain features, obstacles, trenches, etc., are placed only as they become visible, to be captured or bypassed, as ordered. Players would represent a German regimental commander and his subordinates at battalion level. They would be provided with a map (and even air photographs if it can be contrived) but it should also be possible for them to move to other tables, either by accident or design. Model soldiers would be suitable for representing the forces involved, always remembering that a commander's field of vision would be limited. Umpires would play the largely static British defenders, German higher commanders and 'Acts of God'. They would also adjudicate the German players' attempts to communicate, by runner, lights, flares, pigeon and so on.

INDEX

(References to illustrations are shown in **bold**.)